BENTLEY
4½ LITRE

1927 onwards (all models, including 'Blower')

First published in July 2017

A catalogue record for this book is available
from the British Library.

ISBN 978 1 78521 070 9

Library of Congress control no. 2016949313

Published by Haynes Publishing,
Sparkford, Yeovil,
Somerset BA22 7JJ, UK.
Tel: 01963 440635
Int. tel: +44 1963 440635
Website: www.haynes.com

Haynes North America Inc.
859 Lawrence Drive,
Newbury Park, California 91320, USA.

Printed in Malaysia.

Acknowledgements

The authors would like to thank the following: Dr Ian Andrews, Nigel Batchelor (Benjafield's Racing Club), Derek Bell, Alan Bodfish (W.O. Bentley Memorial Foundation), Gerard Brown, the late Michael Burn, Richard Charlesworth (Bentley Motors), Neil Corner, Neil Davies (NDR), Gregor Fisken (Fiskens), Patrick Fitz-Gibbon, Ewen Getley (Kingsbury Racing Shop), Jonathan Gill (MPA), Julian Grimwade, John Mayhead (Hagerty Insurance), Mike Haigh (Bentley Drivers Club), Ciara Harper (Shuttleworth Collection), Doug Hill (National Motor Museum), Harvey Hine, Miles Hutton, Tony Large, Karen Mann (Stanley Mann Racing Team), Nick Mason, William Medcalf (Vintage Bentley Heritage), Stephen Mosley, Graham Moss (R.C. Moss), Shannon Mullen, David Northey, Martin Overington, Bob Petersen (Bob Petersen Engineering), John Pulford (Brooklands Museum), Ben Reynkens (Historic Competition Services), Andrea Seed (Poppyseed Media), Colin Smyrk (NDR), Philip Strickland, Stephanie Sykes-Dunmore (BRDC), Steve Rendle (Haynes Publishing), Wim Van Roy, Gill Wagstaff, Ron Warmington (Bentley Drivers Club), Colin West, and Allan Winn (Brooklands Museum).

BENTLEY
4½ LITRE

1927 onwards (all models, including 'Blower')

Owners' Workshop Manual

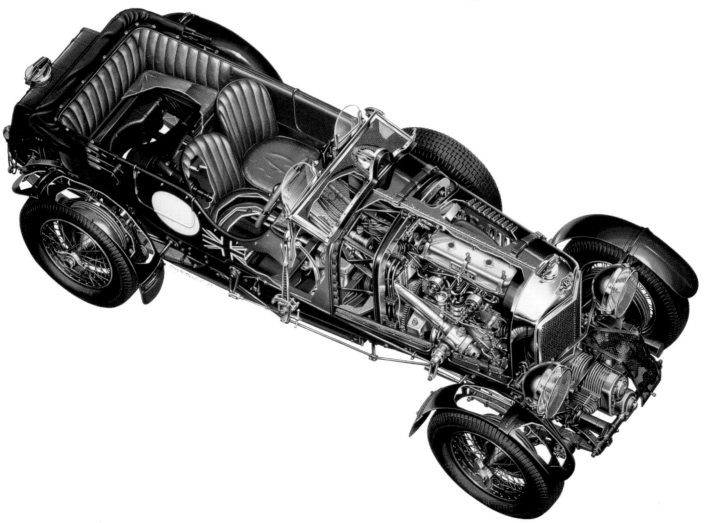

An insight into the design, engineering, maintenance and ownership of W.O. Bentley's legendary Le Mans winner

Andy Brown and Ian Wagstaff

Contents

(Ian Wagstaff)

(Ian Wagstaff)

Chapter One

The Bentley 4½-litre story

The Bentley 4½-litre is surely the most famous of all cars from that marque, its supercharged manifestation the most charismatic. Its fame arguably rests on its racing exploits, particularly at Le Mans, yet its successes were few, the 'blown' version never winning a major race. Yet the thought of one, with 'Tim' Birkin or one of the other 'Bentley Boys' at the wheel, evokes the spirit of the late 1920s like no other racer, and it is as a racing rather than a road car that it is the subject of this book.

OPPOSITE 'Madness, yes, but rather admirable madness.' – Dr J. Dudley Benjafield, Bentley factory driver. *(W.O. Bentley Memorial Foundation)*

The racing history

Although the Bentley marque is now one of the world's most prestigious, and its current owner, Volkswagen AG, continues to allow it to participate in racing, the true spirit of Bentley resides in the 1920s, when success in long-distance racing created a charisma that endures to this day. Although such a car was victorious at Le Mans on only one occasion, the four-cylinder 4½-litre was, arguably, the most charismatic of them all.

In some respects, though, this is a story of two cars. As originally designed, the 4½-litre Bentley was normally aspirated. However, one of the leading drivers in the Bentley team, Sir Henry 'Tim' Birkin, was beguiled by the thought that a supercharger would be the way to challenge the might of the Mercedes SSKs of the era. It is well recorded that W.O. Bentley thoroughly disapproved of the idea, but such a car did makes its debut at the 1929 Brooklands Six Hours and, for the next two years, the 'blown' versions added a lustre to the 4½-litre's name that the conventional cars might not have achieved on their own.

However, the initial Bentley car was a 3-litre that in mock-up form appeared at the 1919 Motor Show. The first of these to go racing did so at Brooklands in 1921 with the company's experienced and optimistic test driver Frank Clement winning his third race with the car, a contest called the ''90 Short', at 87.13mph. Bentleys could be found racing abroad the following year, including in 'of all places' – as company founder W.O. Bentley himself put it – Indianapolis. Douglas Hawkes, unable to stay with the local Miller-engined cars, finished 13th in the annual 500-mile Sweepstakes. Nearer home, Clement, Hawkes and Bentley himself (in his last major race) finished in second, fourth and fifth in the Isle of Man Tourist Trophy, securing the team prize.

The following year, Captain John Duff – whose company Duff & Aldington represented Bentley in the Long Acre area of London – decided that it would be an idea to enter one of the 3-litres for the new Rudge-Whitworth Cup, a biennial affair, the first stage of which would be a 24-hour race just outside what is now the capital of the Sarthe area of France, Le Mans. Despite initial opposition from Bentley

BELOW The Bentley team – a pair of 3-litres and the new 4½-litre – at Newhaven on their way to Le Mans in 1927. *(W.O. Bentley Memorial Foundation)*

himself, Duff with co-driver Clement took fifth place that year, following a series of mishaps as well as a number of record-breaking laps that indicated the car's potential. In 1924 they were back and victorious. The saga of Bentley at Le Mans had begun. Two 3-litre cars were entered the following year and then three in 1926, all of them suffering retirement. A couple of 3-litres were in the line-up for 1927, but now with a significant addition to the ranks, one said to have been designed with the lauded Vauxhall 30/98 in mind: the 4½-litre.

The Bentley 4½-litre at Le Mans

The Le Mans 24 Hours had shown that the 3-litre Bentley was lacking in power by 1927. To remain competitive, the engine was reworked into a 4½-litre. With the prototype, which became known as 'Mother Gun', still under development, the plan was that the 3-litres would still spearhead the racing team. However, such was the progress made on the 4½-litre that it replaced one of the three 3-litre cars entered for Le Mans that year.

'The Bentley entry consists of two cars of the well-known 3-litre type, and a third with a 4-cylinder engine of 100 x 140 mms bore and stroke (4387c.c.),' observed *Motor Sport* magazine. 'This new engine will really consist of 4 cylinders of the 6-cylinder Bentley engine, which has the same bore and stroke.'

Thus, the debut for the 4½-litre Bentley took place at the 1927 Le Mans 24 Hours, a race in which the sole example played merely a supporting role to the 3-litre, 'Old Number Seven', as it became one of the all-time stars of the 24 Hours. Three Bentleys were entered, the new 4½ driven by the head of the company's experimental department, Frank Clement and by Leslie Callingham, plus two 3-litre cars.

Clement led from the start of the race in the new car, to much enthusiastic applause, beating the lap record even with the hood up, the folding roofs being required to be used for the opening laps. Driving beautifully, the car, 'holding the road perfectly' according to *The Motor* magazine, headed the Bentley's two stablemates in what appeared to be an act of domination. Twice Clement set a new lap record for the circuit, his first 13 laps being completed in a time nine minutes shorter than the previous year. The Bentley pit work was also described as 'perfect', Clement himself handling the 4½-gallon cans of fuel in a deft manner. The first stop, at 7:20pm, took 3 minutes 23 seconds, fast for those days. This included slowing away and clipping down the hood, which regulations demanded be up during the opening laps. That took just 35 seconds. By contrast the Bentley's nearest challenger, a large Aries, spent nearly six minutes

ABOVE Hoods up: Clement in the prototype 4½-litre leads the field away at the start of the 1927 Le Mans. *(LAT)*

in the pits. Wrote one of the 3-litre drivers, S.C.H. Davis, later of Clement's pit stop: 'Two hundred and fourteen miles ended, Clement came in, a lap ahead of the 3-litres, downed hood, refilled with that extraordinary speed that even seemed slow to watch, so carefully had every movement been planned by the driver, second to none in the game, handed over to Callingham and came into the pit. There he slid off his visor, a talc screen over the face that I had bought in Paris, where they were sold especially for women motorists, and which proved much better than

goggles to see through in rain, as the air pressure on the curved surface automatically cleared away the water. Wearing one of these and a crash helmet brought back memories of armour in the Tower at once.'

All was going well until dusk. As evening had fallen so the two 3-litre Bentleys had caught up their sister car and the three had then spread out in team order. Then, some time before 10:00pm occurred an accident, which had the potential to be the most disastrous to befall a single team at Le Mans. Callingham, who had now taken over the race-leading 4½-litre, was charging down from Arnage to the grandstands, when, as he arrived at the White House corner – *Maison Blanche* – it was to find a dark blue, 2-litre Th. Schneider sideways across the road. Its driver, Pierre Tabourin, had skidded into the wall when another competitor had passed him, and had bounced back into the middle of the road. Approaching at around 70mph, Callingham made an attempt to skid past the French car but crashed into a ditch on the right-hand side of the road. He was thrown out into the middle of the road but nevertheless struggled to his feet and staggered up the road to warn the following drivers. The 4½-litre rolled over on to the Th. Schneider. A couple more French cars joined the melee, as did George Duller's 3-litre Bentley. This hit the 4½-litre with such force that it threw it back into the road and then fell on it.

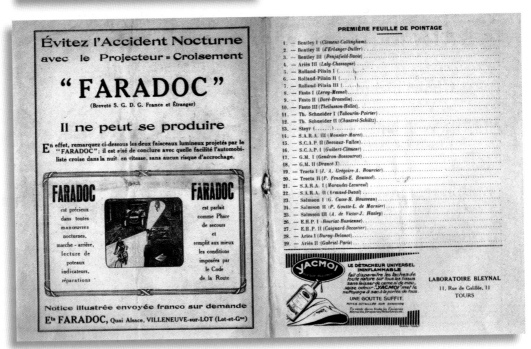

That was it as far as the story of the 4½-litre and the 1927 Le Mans was concerned. However, 'Sammy' Davis was next on the scene in the second of the 3-litres. As he approached the White House, he noticed some splintered wood and a scattering of earth, enough to ring an alarm bell. However, he was not quite prepared to see the 4½-litre rising, as *The Motor* put it 'like some weird monster' from the ditch. The story of how he slid into the mass – bending the front axle well back on the right-hand spring as well as bending the frame, bowing the front cross-tube and sustaining various other damages – and yet went on gallantly to win the race, is outside the scope of this book, but has to be recorded.

Neville Minchin, a noted observer of early motoring, claimed there were only two spectators at the scene of the accident, himself and a Mr Stephenson, who, he said, was 'a grandson of the man to whom we owe the locomotive' (strange, given that there were no direct descendants of George Stephenson and his son Robert). Searching at the scene of the accident, Minchin found the 4½-litre's driver Callingham and asked him what had become of Duller. 'George is very dead, I'm afraid,' was the answer, followed by a voice from the gloom that said 'Oh no I'm not.'

'We laughed in relief,' recalled Minchin. Davis told a similar story although he does not mention Minchin, and it was 'Sammy' himself who asked Duller if he was hurt, to which came the reply – presumably referring to his 3-litre – 'No, but this one's very dead.' So, as far as this race was concerned, was the prototype 4½-litre.

The following year all three Bentleys entered for Le Mans were 4½-litre models, the same

ABOVE The White House debacle. Duller (left) and Callingham's cars face each other in the ditch. *(W.O. Bentley Memorial Foundation)*

BELOW The Birkin/ Chassagne 4½-litre sweeps past the stationary Chrysler of Soffel and Rossingol at Le Mans in 1928. *(W.O. Bentley Memorial Foundation)*

cars that had run in the earlier Six Hours at
Brooklands. Hoods were no longer required but
each car featured an enormous third headlamp.
The old upright windscreens had been replaced
by fold-flat screens moulded to the scuttle line.
The Motor observed that the Bentleys were
'distinctly faster' than the previous year's sole
4½-litre. The opposition had, for the first time,
a transatlantic flavour with a 4.9-litre Stutz
and four 4.1-litre Chryslers to add to France's
lone Aries.

The driver line-up for Bentley was 'Babe'

Barnato/Bernard Rubin, Sir Henry Birkin/Jean
Chassagne and Dr Dudley Benjafield/Frank
Clement. Right from the start it could be seen
that it would not be easy for the team. The lap
record was broken first by the American car,
and then by Barnato and Clement, all within the
first hour. The Aries had retired after only two
laps, as the race turned into an Anglo-American
tussle. The Birkin/Chassagne car headed the
field for the first 20 laps, Barnato/Rubin taking
over as the leader punctured. Then the black
Stutz swept into the lead for the first time,
losing it just one lap later as Barnato returned to
the front for three laps. On lap 27 the Stutz was
once again back in front, where it now remained
for some appreciable time.

Unfortunately, 'W.O.' had made a mistake.
In an effort to lighten his cars as much as
possible, he had instructed that none of
them should carry a jack. 'Tim' Birkin, in
his first Le Mans, ran over a horseshoe nail
as he approached the top of the hill after
Pontlieue. Before he could pull up, the tyre had
disintegrated and the canvas had jammed itself
between the wheel and the brake drum. 'So
there I was,' said the baronet later, 'six miles

from the pits,' and with no jack – 'the only implement of which I was really in need'. Using a hammer, jack knife and a pair of pliers, he set to work and eventually freed the canvas. He was able to continue on, but only as far as Arnage, three miles to go, before the rim collapsed. His next move was to run to the pits, where he arrived 'joints aching'. Only one man, said Birkin, 'had his wits about him,' his 47-year-old co-driver, Jean Chassagne. The Frenchman calmly observed, *'Maintenant, c'est à moi,'* picked up a couple of jacks and ran back to the car. The whole incident cost the pair around three hours, but once on their way again they drove like madmen. Reporting on the above events, *Motor Sport* said that 'probably the finest exhibition of driving and doggedness ever seen over this course was put up by an Englishman on an English car.'

Meanwhile the race continued, with the Stutz leading throughout most of the night followed by the Barnato/Rubin Bentley and one of the Chryslers. The Clement/Benjafield Bentley had been in fourth place but retired with a cracked chassis frame, caused by metal fatigue which had been induced by vibration and led to a radiator hose being pulled away. The team was concerned that the second-place car, now the only Bentley with any chance of winning, might also succumb to the same problem.

On the Sunday afternoon the Stutz lost the lower two of its three gears and Barnato moved into the lead as the American straight-eight was refuelled. The team, though, had been right to assume a weakness in the 4½-litre model's chassis. From the pits it could be seen that the car was beginning to distort in shape, a sign of such a malady. 'Babe' slowed down and nursed it over the last few laps, finishing a mere eight miles ahead of the Stutz. It had been, reported *Motor Sport*, 'one of the finest road races ever staged on the Continent or anywhere else.'

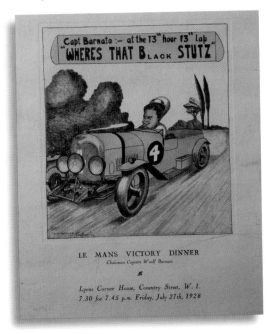

ABOVE The Bentley 4½-litre of Barnato/ Rubin and the Stutz of Brisso/Bloch finished in this order at Le Mans in 1928 after a fierce duel that only ended when the American car lost top gear with an hour and a half left to run. *(W.O. Bentley Memorial Foundation)*

Bentley had won the Le Mans 24 Hours for the second time, the only occasion that a 4½-litre was to come first in the world's most prestigious endurance race. Four would be entered for the following year's contest but they were by then, in Bentley's own words, 'getting short of breath'.

The battle for the lead in 1928 was not the only drama involving a Bentley 4½-litre as the race drew to a close. In the early days, the Le Mans 24 Hours was more a matter of the complex Rudge-Whitworth competition regulations than outright victory. Birkin and

Chassagne has been slashing their way past the now depleted field, but to qualify for the second half of the contest, the following year, they still had to finish within a certain time. With 24 hours nearly up, pit signals were sent to Birkin informing him that he must break the lap record on his final tour if the car was to be back the next year. The pit crew thought this highly unlikely, but 'Tim' responded. His mechanic Chevrollier, hearing the approach of the car for the final time, realised Birkin was going to make it, and with a cry of 'He's done it!' pranced up and

RIGHT The Clement/ Chassagne and Kidston/Dunfee 4½-litres in the pits at Le Mans, 1929. (W.O. Bentley Memorial Foundation)

LEFT The Clement/
Chassagne 4½-litre
blasts down the
Mulsanne Straight
in 1929 on its way to
fourth place.
(W.O. Bentley Memorial
Foundation)

down. It was the first of a hat-trick of fastest laps at Le Mans for Birkin.

Despite the quartet of 4½-litre cars entered in 1929, they were not to win again, victory that year going to the fifth Bentley, a new Speed Six model, which had been entrusted to Barnato and Birkin. It had been hoped to enter two new supercharged 4½-litre cars, the build of which was being masterminded by Birkin, but these were withdrawn because of lubrication troubles. Nevertheless, it was still decided to divide the entry into two teams, the Speed Six and two of the smaller cars managed by 'Nobby'

Clarke, the other two by 'Bertie' Kensington Moir, who was originally slated to look after the supercharged cars. At the wheel of the 4½-litre entries that year were Kidston and Jack Dunfee, Benjafield and d'Erlanger, Clement and Chassagne, and Howe and Rubin. Only the last failed to finish, having been troubled first with spark plugs and then a broken magneto driveshaft before retiring at the end of the afternoon.

The green Bentleys had taken the lead from the start, with only a pair of Stutzes able to keep up with them. The Speed Six, though,

BELOW In the 1929
Le Mans the Clement/
Chassagne 4½-litre
was running second
at half-distance but
dropped back to fourth
after maladies. Its
day was yet to come.
(W.O. Bentley Memorial
Foundation)

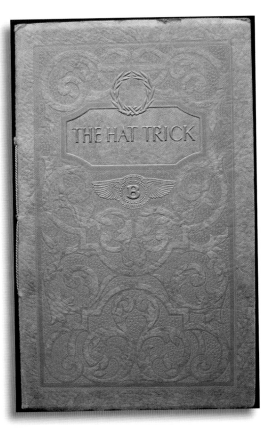

was the future, not the 4½-litre model. The
Bentleys led the race but the six-cylinder car led
the Bentleys. Only ten cars finished, but heading
them all in a procession that was likened to a
squadron of battleships were the four Bentleys,
the leading car also taking the handicap-based
Rudge-Whitworth Cup. There had been a last-
minute concern when it seemed that the whole
team was overdue but it was only because they
had lined up on the Mulsanne Straight to ensure
that they finished together and in the correct
order. Bringing up the rear was the Clement/
Chassagne car, which had led all the other
4½-litres at the halfway point until it became
troubled thanks to shifting balance that snagged
the brakes. (This particular 4½-litre would have
its day at Brooklands later in the year when it
won the 500-mile races there.) The marque had
now won its third consecutive Le Mans, but the
day of the 4½ seemed to be over. However,
one of the Speed Six's two victorious drivers,
'Tim' Birkin, thought differently.

For the poorly attended 1930 race (there

were only 17 starters), the factory team put its complete faith in the Speed Six and arrived with three of these. To their number could now be added a couple of the Birkin-inspired, supercharged 4½-litre cars, entered by the Hon Dorothy Paget but unloved by Bentley himself. (A fourth 'Blower' 4½, as the supercharged Bentleys were popularly known, was entered for Harcourt-Wood and Jack Dunfee but was withdrawn, the official story being it was being saved for the Spa 24 Hour race at the beginning of July.) Bentley, though, needed everything that it could muster from its armoury, for into the fray had come Mercedes-Benz with an SSK driven by the up-and-coming Rudi Caracciola and Christian Werner.

For over half the race the Bentleys harried the white German car, sometimes leading, sometimes not. Birkin, in one of the 'Blowers', was, as had already been agreed by the two teams, particularly aggressive in the opening stages. Indeed, it was the baronet – slightly held up at the start and forced into the gutter

to get past a Stutz – who first wrestled the lead from Caracciola on the fourth lap. In doing so, he shed the offside-rear tyre tread. He flew past the pits with pieces of rubber flying in all directions. It was an anxious lap for the pit crew; a spare wheel and tyre were pushed to the very edge of the counter and team manager Kensington Moir stood ready with a large orange flag. Birkin crawled in, the wheel was quickly changed and he set off after Caracciola. It would not be long before he was less than 11 second behind the German; the next lap he was over five seconds ahead, then they were almost together before tyre trouble hit the Bentley again. 'Tim' observed through the corner of his eye as half of his offside rear wing hurtled through the air, smashed by a flying tyre tread. At Arnage the tyre failed completely, the Bentley turned completely round and Caracciola regained the lead. In those hot early hours, four tyres had to be changed on the 4½-litre, none on the Mercedes-Benz; Birkin and Chassagne dropped back.

BELOW **Birkin was heroic at Le Mans in 1930.** *(W.O. Bentley Memorial Foundation)*

One of the Speed Sixes now took up the challenge. Eventually the Mercedes-Benz failed to restart following a night-time pit stop, the claim being that its dynamo had burnt out. The two 'Blower' 4½-litre cars were also heading for ultimate retirement and both went out of the race in the 21st hour, thus underlining a reputation for unreliability. The Birkin/Chassagne car suffered con-rod failure, its engine having possibly suffered from the forced pace of the early hours. Piston trouble did for the Benjafield/Ramponi car as it thundered past Les Hunaudières. Birkin, though, had taken the outright lap record once again, and who knows just how much his car had helped in Bentley's successful tactics to push the Mercedes to the limit and to its own retirement? For the record Barnato won for a third successive year, partnered on this occasion by Kidston, but now in a Speed Six. Not long after the race Bentley announced that it was withdrawing from racing. Any cars competing from now on would be privately entered.

The glory years were over, but that was not quite it as far of the saga of the 4½-litre Bentleys at La Sarthe was concerned. Anthony Bevan's car, which he shared with Mike Couper, went

LEFT Benjafield
at Pontlieue in the
second of the Paget
'Blowers'. *(W.O. Bentley
Memorial Foundation)*

BELOW Not an
original place for a
Bentley to crash,
Trévoux got as far as
the White House in
1932. *(LAT)*

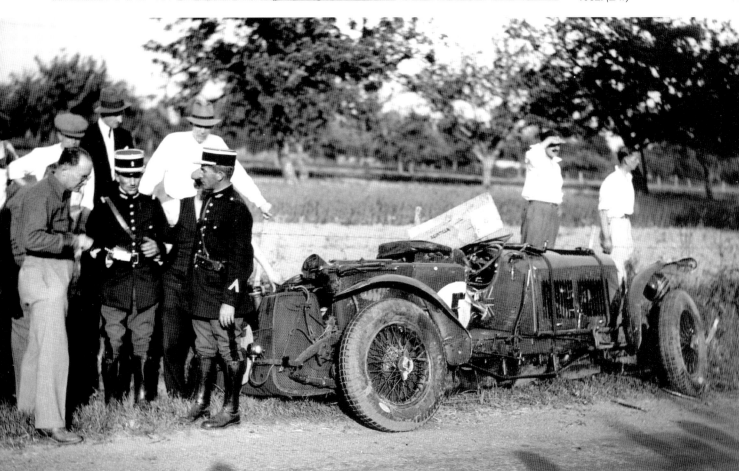

'He could never understand what the fuss was all about,' recalled David Northey and Miles Hutton, the step-grandsons of W.O. (Walter Owen) Bentley. 'His way of being enthusiastic about anything was to say "good".'

And good, when it came to performance, it was. Bentley had already raced both motorcycles and cars before the Great War, notably a French-built DFP with which he made his four-wheel racing debut at the Aston Clinton hill climb in 1912. He did not confine his speed to competition and was stopped on Wimbledon Common for going too fast, although the magistrate threw out the case stating that it was impossible to do 60mph. With his brother, Bentley became UK concessionaire for DFP, as well as Corbin pistons, which he would supply to the Admiralty for use in aircraft engines.

RIGHT A signed photo of 'W.O.' in 1969. *(Patrick Fitz-Gibbon collection)*

BELOW The Bentley rotary-engined Sopwith Snipe was chosen to be the RAF's main line fighter right at the end of the Great War. *(Ian Wagstaff)*

A Royal Naval Air Service officer during the Great War, he was to design a couple of rotary engines, the first, in effect, a superior copy of the French-designed Clerget but with steel-lined aluminium pistons. It was piloting a 230hp B.R.2-engined Sopwith Snipe that Captain William Barker performed one of the greatest feats of aerial combat, taking on a horde of German aeroplanes (some contemporary ground-based reports said 60) single-handed, and shooting down four before eventually crash-landing. Bentley was to say that the 'genesis' of his cars was the engine of the DFP and the Bentley Rotaries.

From the beginning, the modest Bentley wanted to publicise his cars by entering them for what he called 'suitable' races, but that did not include Le Mans. He had 'massive reservations' when John Duff wanted to enter a 3-litre for the inaugural 24 Hours, thinking it a 'ridiculous idea' that no car would survive. However, he lent test driver Frank Clement to the team and, at the last minute, agreed to supervise the pit, which he later described as little more than a tent. A few hours into the event he 'began to realise that this is a race that might have been instituted especially for our benefit'. His enthusiasm quickly grew, and a year later he was describing Le Mans as 'a most important race for us', a sentiment with which his company's board did not necessarily agree. He himself was later to believe that he and his team had become too pleased with themselves. 'It would have been better for our souls if we had not been so successful so early.'

'He was an engineer,' said step-grandson Northey. 'He never professed to be a businessman. And so it was that, although millionaire enthusiast Woolf Barnato stepped in for a while to save Bentley's under-capitalised company, the receiver eventually arrived and it was sold to Rolls-Royce in 1931. Initially constrained by Rolls-Royce, Bentley was able to join Lagonda in 1935 shortly after that marque had achieved it sole victory at Le Mans. It enabled him to again go racing.'

The four-cylinder 4½-litres were just one of the cars designed during W.O.'s time with his eponymous company. He was proud of all but one of them. 'The one car he really disapproved of was the "Blower",' said Northey.

almost unnoticed in 1931, retiring after 295 miles with ignition problems. Frenchman Jean Trévoux entered his ex-Birkin 'Blower' car for the following couple of years. A photo of the start of the 1932 race shows the car still stationary as the Alfa Romeo works team sweeps past. Trévoux's co-driver 'Mary' (Pierre Brousselet) never had the chance to drive it, as the owner, following his tardy start, was involved in a crash at the White House on the first lap. Trévoux, who was wearing a helmet, escaped with facial bruising and a fractured wrist. The following year the car went somewhat further but was retired after 209 laps when new co-driver Louis Gas went into a violent skid that resulted in a bent axle. This time the story of the 4½-litre Bentley at Le Mans really was over. Indeed, it would not be until 2003 that a car bearing the Bentley brand would win the Le Mans 24 Hours again.

The other endurance races

Endurance racing in the late 1920s did not have the cohesion that it enjoys today. Indeed, there would be no World Sports Car Championship until 1953. Each individual race stood or fell on its own merits and there were various ideas about how they should be run. As we have seen, even the Le Mans 24 Hours was not a straightforward race when it first started

but a complex competition that stretched over three years. Even the specialist press was confused and tended to give more credence to the car that had completed the longest distance right from the start. In the British Isles handicapping was often employed even for the most prestigious races, brought about by major disparities in the entries and also a legacy of the way in which Brooklands' mighty banked track had drawn its initial inspiration from horse racing.

There also tended to be a parochial approach, with Bentley focussing its attention on the British Isles. Even if its large cars had been suitable, there was, for example, no incentive for it to enter the classic Italian road races (although Birkin did make enquires about entering the Mille Miglia in 1930). Road racing was just that – competition on the public highway, a pastime banned in the United Kingdom. There was no British track that we would regard as conventional today (Donington did not open until 1931) and, therefore, Bentley had to travel to the lanes of Ireland to race on the roads. Other than that there was only the temple of pre-war British motor sport, Brooklands in Surrey, where the high banking led to a very specific type of competition, mirrored over the Channel at Montlhéry.

As recounted earlier, the Bentley 4½-litre had made its racing debut at Le Mans in 1927. Although damaged in the White House crash

ABOVE The Bentley marque, by then owned by the Volkswagen Group, would not win at Le Mans again until 2003.
(Ian Wagstaff)

there, it was repaired and entered for another 24-hour event that August, the Grand Prix of Paris at Montlhéry. An event that attracted minimal public interest, this took place over the facility's full road circuit and half a lap of its banked track, a configuration that, unlike Le Mans, did not really suit the Bentley. However, perhaps attracted by the prize money of 34,000 francs, the factory took the event seriously, sending a full complement of mechanics as well as Frank Clement and George Duller as the drivers. There were only 18 starters, the majority local 1,100cc sports cars. As the only contender in the over 2-litre class, the Bentley, despite the nature of the circuit, had virtually no competition. There was none of the running across the road and erecting the hood as at Le Mans; instead, as it does today at La Sarthe, it commenced with a rolling start behind a pace car. There was none of today's precision, though, and Clement fell back into the middle of the pack as the flag fell. This was largely irrelevant, as he was well in the lead by the end of the first lap.

When the rains came down what few spectators there were left, but the Bentley continued to dominate until about midday. It was then that a long fishtail, which had been fitted to the exhaust pipe in order to provide clearance underneath the oval-shaped tank, broke up, and the exhaust flames set light to the coconut matting beneath the tank.

With the rear of his car seemingly on fire, Clement pulled into the pits to be met by a battery of fire extinguishers. At the suggestion of mechanic Wally Hassan the exhaust pipe was cut back and the rear floorboards removed so that any flames could be quickly noticed. It was probably not Hassan's best idea, for although the car was able to continue on its way the driver now found himself being gassed by the fumes that were being sucked in to the car … and the fire restarted. This time Hassan made an effective repair by pointing the end of the exhaust down on to the track. This worked, but the 4½-litre had lost nearly an hour. Did this matter? Not a bit, for the lead had been so great that it was still ahead and finished 11 of the 7.75-mile laps ahead of the little BNC that came second. The 4½-litre had scored its maiden win and, even if the competition had been derisory, it was still good for publicity. There was to be no trophy, though. Hardly any spectators meant no profit for the organisers, who had scarpered with the prize money, as well as the trophies, before the race had ended.

Despite the unfortunate ending, *Motor Sport* had no doubts as to the significance of the result when it came to what it referred to as 'touring car races'. 'The sequel to [the Le Mans win] in the form of the victory won by the 4½-litre car in the Paris Grand Prix and Montlhéry has proved to the hilt the present eminence of Great Britain in this field of activity.'

The next race for the prototype 4½-litre was a very different affair, a class/fuel consumption handicap run over 150 miles at Brooklands.

A couple of 3-litres were also entered for the event, which was co-promoted by the Junior Car Club and the Surbiton Motor Club. As Dr Ian Andrews, the current owner of the 1929 BRDC 500-mile-winning 4½-litre points out, 'Bentley was to win more races at the Weybridge track that any other marque. Had it not been for the experimental and developmental work that was undertaken by Bentley Motors on this circuit, the marque would not have achieved so much at Le Mans during the 1920s.'

Although dominated by a giant, 2.75-mile steeply banked oval, the roads at Brooklands gave the opportunity for a variety of circuits. For the 4½-litre's debut the course was an unusual one, involving the Byfleet Banking, the Finishing and Railway Straights and an oil-drum hairpin. Woolf Barnato was the driver this time, while the car had been specially fitted with an 18-gallon tank from the 3-litre model. 'Babe' set the fastest lap, but with the Austin Sevens given a 1 hour and 54 seconds start he could only come third. Consuming 8.45mpg, he had managed to finish with a mere pint of fuel in the Bentley's tank.

By the autumn of 1927 the first customers were starting to take delivery of their 4½-litre models. Thus plans for the following year's racing centred around the new car, with the original 'Mother Gun' being joined by two

production models, KM3077 and KM3088, in the factory team. The 4½-litre was beginning to take on the look that is so well known today. New Vanden Plas bodywork was fitted and cycle mudguards replaced the long side-wings of the 3-litres. 'Mother Gun'

remained more or less unchanged, but the two new cars appeared with 'bobtails'.

The Six-Hour race at a Brooklands complete with chicanes, which were marked by sandbags and bunting, could be seen as a rehearsal for the coming season with three 4½-litre cars entered. The event was a 46-entry handicap affair, although there was a secondary prize, the Barnato Cup, for the car covering the longest distance. Although the main prize went to an Alfa Romeo 6C-1500, the Bentleys finished first, second and third on distance, with the relatively inexperienced Birkin driving single-handed to take the Barnato Cup. There was also the McReady Cup for the best team. This was another race where hoods had to be up for the initial laps and it is noteworthy that the Bentley drivers were the fastest in erecting theirs. The riding mechanics, though, had to work hard to prevent them from blowing away once the race had begun. Perhaps it was significant that hoods were not required at Le Mans that year.

Said French 24-hour race followed, after which Birkin took his repaired 4½-litre to a hot and crowded Nürburgring, there to single-handedly face five 7-litre supercharged Mercedes-Benz SSs, as well as a gaggle of Bugattis that were, effectively, Grand Prix machines. Accompanied by Wally Hassan as riding mechanic, 'Tim' was the first Englishman

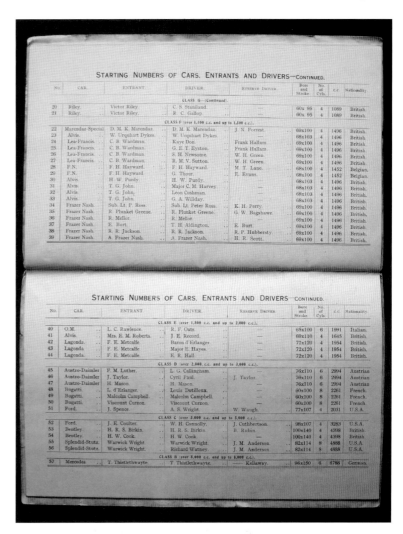

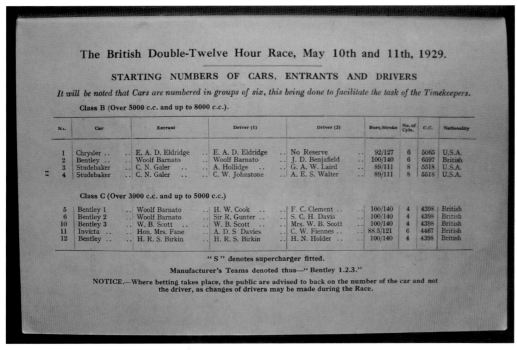

B.A.R.C. "Six Hours" Endurance Race, 29th June, 1929.
Starting numbers of Cars, Entrants and Drivers.

Class B. (Over 5,000 c.c. and up to 8,000 c.c.)

No.	Car.	Entrant.	Driver (1).	Driver (2).	Bore/Stroke.	No. of Cyls.	c.c.
1	Mercédès S.	T. Thistlethwayte	T. Thistlethwayte	L. A. R. Braddell	100/150	6	7,100
2	Mercédès S.	J. E. P. Howey	J. E. P. Howey	No Reserve	98/150	6	6,800
3	Bentley	Woolf Barnato	Woolf Barnato	J. Barclay	100/140	6	6,597

Class C. (Over 3,000 c.c. and up to 5,000 c.c.)

No.	Car.	Entrant.	Driver (1).	Driver (2).	Bore/Stroke.	No. of Cyls.	c.c.
4	Bentley	Woolf Barnato	Kaye Don	H. W. Cook	100/140	4	4,398
5	Bentley S.	H. R. S. Birkin	H. R. S. Birkin	No Reserve	100/140	4	4,398
6	Bentley	H. N. Holder	H. N. Holder	B. Rubin	100/140	4	4,398
7	Bentley	W. B. Scott	W. B. Scott	J. Patterson	100/140	4	4,398

Class D. (Over 2,000 c.c. and up to 3,000 c.c.)

No.	Car.	Entrant.	Driver (1).	Driver (2).	Bore/Stroke.	No. of Cyls.	c.c.
8	Bugatti S.	R. Wyndham	R. Wyndham	G. D. Erler	60/100	8	2,300
9	Austro-Daimler	K. Eggar	K. Eggar	No Reserve	76/110	6	2,994
10	Lagonda	A. W. Fox	F. King	No Reserve	72/120	6	2,931
11	Lagonda	A. W. Fox	J. S. Hindmarsh	No Reserve	72/120	6	2,931

"S" denotes supercharger fitted.

Class E. (Over 1,500 c.c. and under 2,000 c.c.)

No.	Car.	Entrant.	Driver (1).	Driver (2).	Bore/Stroke.	No. of Cyls.	c.c.
12	Lagonda	R. S. S. Hebeler	R. S. S. Hebeler	I. Hepburn	72/120	4	1,954
14	Lagonda	W. M. Couper	W. M. Couper	No Reserve	72/120	4	1,954
15	Lagonda	A. W. Fox	T. E. Rose-Richards	C. J. Randall	72/120	4	1,954
16	Lagonda	A. W. Fox	G. Roberts	A. A. Pollard	72/120	4	1,954
17	Lagonda	A. W. Fox	H. F. Wolfe	No Reserve	72/120	4	1,954
18	Lagonda	A. W. Fox	R. R. Jackson	C. A. Broomhall	72/120	4	1,954
20	O.M.	M. C. Morris	A. V. Wilkinson	S. G. Ormsby	65/100	6	1,991
21	O.M.	L. C. Rawlence	R. F. Oats	No Reserve	65/100	6	1,991
22	Alfa-Romeo S.	J. D. Benjafield	J. D. Benjafield	B. Ivanowsky	65/88	6	1,750
23	Alfa-Romeo S.	L. Headlam	L. Headlam	W. Headlam	65/88	6	1,750

Class F. (Over 1,100 c.c. and under 1,500 c.c.)

No.	Car.	Entrant.	Driver (1).	Driver (2).	Bore/Stroke.	No. of Cyls.	c.c.
24	Alfa-Romeo S.	G. E. T. Eyston	G. E. T. Eyston	E. Fronteras	62/82	6	1,494
25	Frazer-Nash S.	A. M. Conan-Doyle	A. M. Conan-Doyle	R. G. Nash	69/100	4	1,496
26	Frazer-Nash	N. Jupp	N. Jupp	No Reserve	69/100	4	1,496
27	Frazer-Nash	E. Burt	Capt. A. Fraser Nash	S. G. Burt	69/100	4	1,496
30	Lea-Francis S.	R. Childe	R. Childe	J. Bidmead	69/100	4	1,496
31	Lea-Francis S.	H. R. Wellsteed	E. Thomas	H. R. Wellsteed	69/100	4	1,496
32	Lea-Francis S.	Gordon Hendy	Gordon Hendy	T. Owen Hodder	69/100	4	1,496
33	Lea-Francis S.	S. H. Newsome	G. L. Jackson	S. H. Newsome	69/100	4	1,496
34	Lea-Francis S.	S. H. Newsome	W. H. Green	S. H. Newsome	69/100	4	1,496
35	Lea-Francis S.	K. Peacock	K. Peacock	S. H. Newsome	69/100	4	1,496
36	Lea-Francis S.	Hon. Mrs. Chetwynd	Hon. A.D. Chetwynd	A. N. L. Maclachlan	69/100	4	1,496
37	Alvis S.	N. A. Carr	N. A. Carr	No Reserve	68/102	4	1,482

"S" denotes supercharger fitted.

to compete at the forbidding circuit. The conditions were demanding – leader Rudi Caracciola pitted with heat exhaustion – but Birkin seemed unaffected as he drove to an eighth-place finish. Against the power of the Mercedes and the nimbleness of the Bugattis, the conventional 4½-litre was not a match. However, Birkin had now experienced Caracciola and the supercharged German cars, and this was to have an effect on him.

If it had not been for Birkin the 4½-litre would have virtually disappeared from the racing scene following Le Mans. However, after the Nürburgring, Sir Henry headed for Ireland and the Ards circuit. When W.O. learnt that the revived Tourist Trophy would be a handicap affair, he withdrew the factory team – after all, the Bentleys would have to make up four laps on the smallest cars and he felt a victory was out of the question (*Motor Sport* begged to differ, saying his cars 'had the very good chance of winning the race despite the handicap'). Not that Bentley's view deterred Birkin. He entered his faithful car, now with a standard rather than a bobtail, and was joined by Humphrey Cook, who had just purchased a new 4½-litre built to the same specification as the factory cars, this being the car that would later win the inaugural BRDC 500-miles. These two were not the only 4½-litres present that day, the course being closed prior to the race by former Sunbeam driver Kenelm Lee Guinness in such a car before Brooklands' famed timekeeper 'Ebby' Ebblewhite sent the cars off with a wave of an enormous red flag.

Dr Ian Andrews, who has taken his very original 4½-litre back to Ireland on a number of occasions, observes that the course itself was described by Birkin as being shaped 'like a kite' having three principal corners named after their respective villages, Newtownards, Comber and Dundonald, the last with its famous hairpin. Earl Howe wrote, 'Most famous of all the circuits … Ards is a real, genuine road circuit, better than any of those on the Continent.' Spectator numbers for the 1928 race were estimated to have been something between a half and three-quarters of a million.

The Bentleys, perhaps not surprisingly, led the field until both were temporarily halted to repair broken oil pipes. By half-distance they were again well ahead of the field but to no avail – the handicap set was too draconian. Birkin was finally classified in fifth place, winning the unlimited class in the process, Cook in seventh. Three weeks later Birkin was in Boulogne for the Coupe George Boillot, another handicap affair which again proved too much and he was again classified as fifth.

The period during which the 4½-litre car was the factory's weapon of choice was a small one. By the end of 1928 the Speed Six had been shown to the world. Birkin, Bentley Motors and Amherst Villiers had also signed their agreement to develop a supercharged version. Meanwhile, W.O.'s plans revolved around the 6½-litre car although, thanks to a Le Mans Replica of the smaller car being made available to the public, there were four 4½-litres entered for the innovative Brooklands Double Twelve the next May. Run as a handicap over two chunks

of 12 hours (night-time racing was forbidden at Brooklands), the result was in doubt even a quarter of an hour after the finish. Eventually, though, the timekeepers awarded first place to an Alfa Romeo. A mere 0.003 on the handicap formula separated this from one of the 4½-litres, that of 'Sammy' Davis and Roland Gunter, which had suffered from a rear tyre breaking up in the last half hour. Again the Bentley had fallen foul of the handicapper.

It was during this race that Birkin brought into the pits a 4½-litre that he was sharing with its owner, Nigel Holder. Mechanic Chevrollier spilt fuel over both himself and the exhaust. The unburnt gases in the exhaust system exploded, although the engine had been switched off for about half a minute, and Chevrollier was badly burnt. From then on Bentley drivers were instructed to switch off their engines some way out before stopping at the pits. Team manager 'Bertie' Kensington Moir also took to throwing a bucket of water over the tail pipe as the car came to a halt.

Following playing second fiddle to the Speed Six at Le Mans, the 4½-litre cars were back at Brooklands for the Six-Hour race, which had been taken over from the defunct Essex Club by the BARC. It was to be yet another of the handicap events so beloved at Brooklands, but this time Bentley – albeit a Speed Six – was not to be denied. Humphrey Cook and Leslie Callingham came home third in the former's 4½-litre, which was entered as a works car. The significance of this event, though, was the entry by Birkin of the first 'Blower' 4½-litre to be completed – on the morning of the race, in fact – at his Welwyn Garden City works. It was not, though, an auspicious beginning, as the need to replace a supercharger release-valve spring meant a long pit stop after the car had, admittedly, shown considerable speed.

A week later and the scene had moved back across the sea for the inaugural Irish Grand Prix at Phoenix Park, Dublin. This was another handicap contest which, to make matters even more confusing, was run in two parts – separate races for the up to and over 1,500cc cars. Phoenix Park was one of the fastest racing circuits in Europe at the time, observes Dr Andrews, with a straight of two miles between the Mountjoy and Gough Memorial

Corners and the remaining two miles curving back again like the round stroke of a capital 'D'. As with the Ards TT circuit, the track remains as it was back in 1929.

Two blown Bentleys headed a list of seven cars from the marque. Birkin finished third with an overheating engine, beaten by one of those Alfas and teammate Kidston in a Speed Six but ahead of another four 4½-litre cars, the last of which was a troubled Bernard Rubin in a second 'Blower'. As far as Birkin was concerned, further development of the 'Blowers' was fully justified; Barnato had given the project his blessing and W.O. was finding it difficult to maintain his objections.

The number of 'Blowers' had risen to three when the cars moved into the north of Ireland for the Tourist Trophy, again to be held on the Ards circuit. Beris Harcourt-Wood, driving the prototype, had joined Birkin and Rubin in the ranks. A fourth, unblown 4½-litre was also entered, this being 'Mother Gun', now owned by Richard Norton and driven by the inexperienced 'Frothblower' Hayes. Being the

riding mechanic to any of these was to be heroic or foolhardy. Quite which is open to question, but when Birkin suggested in jest to W.O. that he should replace regular mechanic Chevrollier in the left-hand seat, he agreed. Team manager Kensington Moir was aghast, but W.O. managed to get over life insurance problems and that was that. It nearly did not happen, though, as Birkin sportingly threatened to withdraw his cars unless the Mercedes team, the exhausts of which the scrutineers were unhappy about, were allowed to race.

Following an exciting event, Birkin, with an impassive Bentley by his side, finished second-fastest but was classified in 11th; yes, it was another handicap contest. Having said that, Caracciola had proved that large cars could win on handicap with his Mercedes-Benz.

Harcourt-Wood retired for sundry reasons while Rubin crashed, he and his mechanic being pinned underneath the car and possibly escaping unscathed only because of the strength of the car's Harrison body.

The long-distance season finished for

BELOW Birkin and 'Blower' at Phoenix Park. *(W.O. Bentley Memorial Foundation)*

Bentley back at Brooklands for the inaugural British Racing Drivers' Club 500-mile race ('the first really long distance purely track race for cars held in this country for many years'), and further proof to W.O. that a large car *could* win a handicap race. The 1928 Le Mans apart it was also, arguably, the 4½-litre's finest hour. Unlike its Indianapolis namesake, the race would be a handicap but would use the steeply banked Outer Circuit. The cars were flagged off at intervals meaning that all would have to aim for the full 181 laps. Five Bentleys were on the lists, all but one 4½-litre cars although only the entry of Birkin and Harcourt-Wood was supercharged. The factory entered Humphrey Cook's unblown YW 5758 to be driven by Frank Clement and Jack Barclay, who had a Bentley agency in Mayfair, London. A streamlined tail had been fitted and the passenger seat and rear compartment fared in. This was not a sports car race, so the mudguards and lights were also removed. The result cannot be said to have been a thing of beauty but it was to prove effective. Birkin's car also had an altered appearance, having jettisoned its Harrison body for one from Vanden Plas.

Such was the handicapping that it seemed the smallest cars would be difficult to catch up. In trying to do so Barclay had a lurid spin on the Members' Banking, finishing up near the rim of the banking. It appears that this was not a lesson learnt, for he later repeated the feat, again on the Members' Banking, this time really courting disaster when his offside wheels went off the edge. Barclay ducked down, fearing the worst, but the Bentley recovered. As before he immediately stopped at the pits, but this time Frank Clement took over. Frank's professional driving ability was clear as he circulated steadily, picking off the smaller cars and moving into the lead. There he remained until the end, followed by Davis who had been having an entertaining time in the 6½-litre 'Old Number One'. Birkin, who along with Davis and Clive Dunfee were awarded BARC 120mph badges for their lap speeds, fell foul of an exhaust joint which had already met with W.O.'s disapproval, his car's bodywork fabric catching fire when it broke.

Watching the race had been the 24-year-old Hon Dorothy Paget, heiress to an American banking fortune. Birkin, who had been financing the supercharged cars himself, had now run out of money, but in stepped the eccentric Paget, whose interest really lay in racehorses. Following the 500-miles she put in enough

money to keep Birkin's Welwyn Garden City operation going, also buying his four racing cars. As far as Bentley was concerned, though, the 4½-litre model was now obsolete. The factory would enter only two major endurance races in 1930, in both cases using 6½-litre cars.

One of the now Paget blown cars was converted into a single-seater, of which more anon. Birkin also explored the possibility of taking a 'Blower' to the Mille Miglia but logistical problems proved too great. The single-seater was already becoming a familiar sight at

BELOW Brooklands remains a magnet for 4½-litre Bentleys. Sati Lall's was just one that drove from the relaunch of William Medcalf's Vintage Bentley Heritage showroom to the track in January 2017. *(Ian Wagstaff)*

Brooklands by the time of the JCC Double Twelve, for which three conventional Paget Team 'Blowers' were entered along with an independent unblown car. It was at this meeting that John Cobb, who was to become the ultimate holder of the Brooklands Outer Circuit lap record as well as Land Speed Record holder, so nearly became one of the Bentley Boys. Birkin wanted him to drive one of the 'Blowers', but negotiations proved complex.

As it was, while the Speed Sixes swept on to first and second places, not one of the 4½-litre cars managed to finish the race, although they were reported as setting a terrific pace at the outset. The Paget cars then failed again at Le Mans, as reported above, albeit making history in the process. The factory now withdrew from racing, leaving Paget's supercharged 4½-litre cars to fly the proverbial flag. *Motor Sport* rather overoptimistically stated that it had 'learnt from Bentleys that there is no question but that should this country start to lose her lead in this particular class, they will return to the fray in full force, and in the meantime they will be giving

BELOW Birkin's 'Blowers' head the line-up for the 1930 Brooklands Double Twelve. Hand on hip in the bottom right-hand corner of the photograph, W.O. ponders on the possible result.
(W.O. Bentley Memorial Foundation)

every assistance and encouragement to any private entrants. In other words we can look to Birkin and his team of "Blower" Bentleys to keep their end up.' Easier written than done.

It was now time to return to Ireland, the next two races being the Irish Grand Prix and the RAC Tourist Trophy, again both handicap contests. Birkin fought hard at Phoenix Park – where Caracciola, who started two laps after him, had his revenge – eventually finishing fourth in a rain-affected race, with the other two Paget cars unclassified. Dorothy Paget was losing interest. However, she again entered a trio of cars for the TT, where Eddie Hall also entered with his unblown 4½-litre. Birkin crashed into a stone wall at Ballystock, his only accident while racing a Bentley, and 'Bertie' Kensington Moir – competing for the first time since 1925 – was first of the Bentleys, back in 11th place. Birkin was unhurt but Paget had had enough and said it would be the last race that she would support.

It is a cliché that nobody remembers who came second. Yet, as far as the 1930 Grand Prix de l'ACF is concerned, it is more likely that it is the winner who is forgotten. This was to be Birkin and the 'Blower's' finest hour.

It was an unusual situation. A fuel formula was then in existence for Grands Prix but this attracted hardly any entries for the French Grand

ABOVE Eddie Hall's unblown 4½-litre (No 4) follows away the three Paget cars at the 1930 Tourist Trophy.
(Dr Ian Andrews collection)

RIGHT Birkin presses on during the 1930 TT.
(W.O. Bentley Memorial Foundation)

BELOW **A fast bend under Ballystockart railway bridge caught Birkin out during the 1930 TT; his nearside front hub hit a telegraph pole, tearing off a tyre, the car spinning before hitting a wall. It was Birkin's only crash in a Bentley, although he and mechanic Whitlock were unhurt.** *(W.O. Bentley Memorial Foundation)*

Prix, as the Grand Prix de l'ACF was better known. Thus it was decided to run the race as a *Formule Libre* event and delay it until the September. That meant a clash with the Czech GP and the absence of the Italian teams, leaving a field mainly consisting of Bugattis. The only non-French entry was greeted with derision, it being Birkin's No 4 supercharged 4½-litre – equivalent to an LMP1 being entered today against a field of Formula One cars. It was, said Sir Henry, 'among the greyhounds a large Sealyham', although *Motor Sport* reckoned that

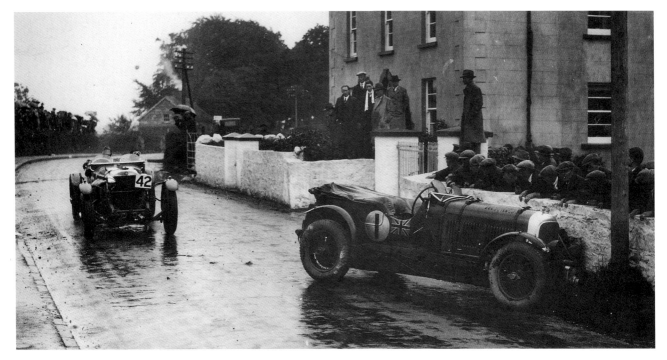

Dorothy Paget, the daughter of English aristocrat Lord Queenborough, and an American heiress, is said to have been worth the equivalent of what would now be £100 million; but, as is said, money is not everything. Much has been made of her plain looks, increasing weight, humourless nature and addiction to gambling. However, she was described in the press at the time as 'one of the finest women drivers of fast cars'.

To the outside world she is best remembered for her involvement in a somewhat slower form of racing, that for horses, but at the age of 24 became one of the most significant players in the story of the supercharged 4½-litre Bentley. 'Tim' Birkin had initially been funding the development of these himself but the money had run out. Somehow, despite Paget's aversion to men, Birkin managed to persuade her to finance his team, a decision she is said to have taken after watching the BRDC 500-miles.

Paget's fortune stimulated Birkin's Welwyn-based operation, enabling an increase in the size of its staff and the establishment of a fully equipped machine shop. At one 1930 Brooklands meeting she acted a passenger to Birkin in the Mountain Speed Handicap. She became the official entrant whenever the Birkin-inspired 'Blower' Bentleys raced. In practice for the Irish Grand Prix Malcolm Campbell was another to 'chauffeur' the Hon Dorothy, setting the fastest time in his Mercedes SS despite her bulk. For a while her involvement was such that at one August Bank Holiday Brooklands meeting she entered Birkin in what had become the single-seater 'Blower' Bentley as well as in a 1924 GP Mercedes, plus Jack Dunfee in a Mercedes SS. Following the 1930 Tourist Trophy, Paget told Birkin that it would be the last time she would support the team. However, she was still the entrant at the forthcoming BRDC 500-miles and continued to back him in the single-seater at Brooklands after that.

Following Birkin's death the eccentric and volatile Paget returned to her first love, becoming a particularly noted breeder and owner of racehorses, keeping strange hours and her trainers forever on their toes. One of her horses, Golden Miller, was highly successful, winning the Cheltenham Cup on five consecutive occasions and in 1934 achieving the unique double of the Gold Cup and the Grand National. She died of heart failure in 1960.

RIGHT Birkin and Paget, on this occasion a passenger in one of her cars, study form at Brooklands. *(W.O. Bentley Memorial Foundation)*

it 'should have a very good chance'. The wings, headlights and other touring impedimenta were removed and the four-seater car was entered against some of the finest Grand Prix machines that France could offer. The incongruity of it all was underlined when Birkin used his horn to persuade leading Bugatti driver Louis Chiron to move over. Yet only one Bugatti remained ahead of the Bentley at the end of the race; nothing should detract from this performance. However, because of the tight confines of the very different street track that came to be used for the later Pau Grand Prix, an idea has emerged that Birkin had wrestled a most unsuitable machine (Ettore Bugatti had described the Bentleys as 'trucks') around a twisting track. But the route used for the 1930 race was outside the city and could have been described as almost Le Mans-like in character. Certainly its long straights assisted the supercharged Bentley. However, a photograph taken of Birkin in the car just after the race shows the strain he must have been under.

'The crowd laugh at your Bentley, *Capitaine* Birkin,' observed Charles Faroux, one of the founders of the Le Mans 24 Hours, 'but I tell them not to laugh. I have seen the Bentleys at Le Mans and I know. I am Faroux. I am not a [...] fool.'

And the winner, as if it now matters? Philippe Etancelin curbed his youthful impulsiveness, and with his fuel dangerously low and nursing a sick clutch, managed to hold off Birkin, who was slowly chasing him down over the final five laps.

Despite her earlier comment, Paget was to retain the single-seater. This, along with two of her conventional cars, was entered for the BRDC 500-mile handicap, which again ended the Brooklands season. Dudley Benjafield chased one of the little Austins hard but eventually he and Eddie Hall had be content with second place, a troubled Birkin and George Duller being classified further back in ninth in the single-seater. The latter car was back for the 1931 500-miles but not with Birkin at the wheel. On this occasion his good friend Dudley Benjafield was the driver, while Couper and Bevan shared an unblown 4½-litre as they did at Le Mans that year. The single-seater popped and banged around for ten laps before being retired, while the Le Mans car kept going to the end.

ABOVE 'A large
Sealyham'.
*(W.O. Bentley Memorial
Foundation)*

The day of the factory and Paget 4½-litre sports cars, though, was now over, as far as the classic races were concerned. As recounted, privately entered models continued to race at Le Mans up to 1933, while a couple were entered for the 1931 BRDC 500-miles. The final appearance of a 4½-litre was at the same event three years later. No 4½-litre was classified as a finisher during this time. A legend had been created but it had really come to an end in late 1930.

Lesser events

Motor racing opportunities were limited in the late 1920s and early 1930s and, away from the classic events, the Bentleys tended to be confined to Brooklands and the then popular sport of speed hill climbing when it came to lesser events. While these leviathans were palpably suited to the great Weybridge bowl, they must have appeared out of place on the narrow confines of hill climbs. Nevertheless, the 4½-litre Bentley slotted into the traditional fare of British motor sport well. Its first success, as such, came in the Inter-Varsity Speed Trial of 1928, which was held at the 1,240-yard Ewelme Down near Wallingford in Oxfordshire, where a Vanden Plas-bodied version won the touring class and also came third in the racing class, driven by T.G. Moore. The future *Motor Sport* editor, driving for the losing Oxford team, was 'very fast and very spectacular'. A year

by a lady driving a sports car of unlimited capacity'. At the following year's open, Eddie won the President's Cup for the fastest time of the day by a 'British sports car of any capacity' with a time of 51.8 seconds, over six seconds quicker than his wife's time of the year before. He was also presented with the Garvagh Challenge Cup for the 'fastest time by a sports car over 1500cc'. One has to presume that this was an award for the locals, as one Rudi Caracciola set a new sports car record for Shelsley that day with a run of 46.4 seconds. Mrs Hall drove the Bentley as part of the Midlands Automobile Club set-up that won the Team Event at the September event, husband Eddie also a member of the team but now at the wheel of a Vauxhall.

Brooklands, though, was where the Bentley 4½-litre was more likely to shine, Hall, for example, winning the Mountain Handicap at its 1930 Whitsun meeting. Rubin and Barnato were entering such cars there – the latter's driven by Dudley Froy – for minor events as early as 1928, with others following the next year. Froy also set new world records for the 200 kilometres and 200 miles, as well as various Class C records with the car at Brooklands in October 1928.

Another banked track, Montlhéry near Paris, also saw Bentley 4½-litre activity in 1929 with Mildred (the Hon Mrs Victor) Bruce taking Birkin's car from the Double Twelve

ABOVE The Hon Mrs Victor Bruce's car is refuelled at Montlhéry. Fire risk, what fire risk? *(W.O. Bentley Memorial Foundation)*

later he wrote: 'The cornering was found to be very good though we never felt able to be quite as brutal on corners as we had been with our first Bentley, and the greater weight and slightly different steering, were probably responsible. However, the road-holding on the straight more than compensated for this.'

In 1929 we find Eddie Hall's 4½-litre entered at the famed Shelsley Walsh hill climb in Worcestershire. At the open meeting there, it was Hall's first wife Evelyn who won the first trophy for the car, the quaintly named *Good Housekeeping* Cup for the 'best performance

RIGHT In an end-of-season rush for records at Brooklands, Dudley Froy in 'Blower' Bentley found himself alongside the Rex-Acme of M.V. McCudden, the brother of the late James McCudden VC, one of the leading fighter pilots of World War One. *(W.O. Bentley Memorial Foundation)*

there to run single-handedly for 24 hours. The car was crashed on the way to the track by BP representative Harold Parker, the run was delayed by poor weather and she even took a swig of petrol by mistake, but still covered a record-breaking 2,164 miles at an average speed of 89.57mph. The French track was also used in 1930 and 1931 to claim a variety of other Class C records for the 4½-litre, Froy again being one of the drivers.

While the majority of 4½-litre Bentleys racing at Brooklands still looked like touring cars, even if they would sometimes have wings and headlights removed, there was one that stood out as a pure racer. During the winter of 1929/30 the No 1 Team Car from Birkin's 'Blower' line-up was rebuilt using a Reid Railton-designed, initially blue single-seater body. Despite Dorothy Paget's threat to withdraw from racing, she retained this car and entered it for Birkin to drive in the opening meeting of Brooklands' 1930 season, its first race being the Kent Short Handicap. Perhaps not surprisingly it was on scratch, but 'Tim' still managed to finish second. The car ran in four races that day, Birkin winning the Kent Long Handicap, after which, much to his disgust, his handicap was revised and he withdrew from his fourth race shortly after starting.

Nevertheless, the single-seater became a great attraction on the oval. Track historian Bill Boddy reckoned it was developed into 'one of the most exciting outer-circuit cars seen at Brooklands'. A second victory followed shortly afterwards at the Easter meeting when the single-seater became the fastest car on the track during a three-lap match race against Jack Dunfee's GP Sunbeam. The car, which was repainted red for 1932, continued to be run in the shorter handicap races, as well as being entered in the BRDC 500-miles (see page 35). An experiment with a Powerplus supercharger had proved a failure and the original Amherst Villiers blower had now been replaced.

It was a dramatic machine, made all the more so when the auxiliary petrol tank caught fire one day as Birkin was coming off the Byfleet Banking. A well-known photo shows him standing up in the cockpit to avoid the flames as the car comes to a stop. In practice for the 1932 Easter meeting, Birkin was able to set a

new lap record of 137.96mph, winning one of the longer handicap races at that event despite skidding down the banking at one point. The car was entered for the Avusrennen in Berlin and also for the Eifelrennen at the Nürburgring a week later, but although Birkin was present at the AVUS track the car was not. Perhaps the most dramatic win that year was during the August Bank Holiday meeting in a three-lap, 100-sovereign match race against John Cobb's V12 Delage. Thrown around 'in terrifying fashion', 'Tim' caught Cobb on the line to win by 0.2 seconds.

That meeting was the single-seater's last in competition, its final race being the Hereford Lighting Long Handicap when it finished second, 0.6 seconds behind Richard Shuttleworth's Bugatti. It was estimated that Birkin had covered over 500 laps of Brooklands in it. Twice it had beaten the lap record during that period, despite the fact that Birkin, as was stated in his ghost-written autobiography *Full Throttle*, had little love for the track. Following the then Sir Henry's death in 1933, Dorothy Paget appears to have been loath to part with the single-seater, retaining the car for another six years.

More conventional, privately owned 4½-litre Bentleys continued to race at Brooklands during the 1930s, with, for example, the 1929 BRDC 500-miles winner contesting the Somerset Junior Long Handicap and the Gold Star Handicap on Whit Monday 1931 driven and

ABOVE The Paget single-seater 'Blower', seen here being driven by Birkin in the 1932 British Empire Trophy, became a major attraction at Brooklands.
(W.O. Bentley Memorial Foundation)

entered by John Carlson, while Joe Turner won the Addlestone Senior Long Handicap at the 1933 BARC Easter meeting, having bought the prototype 'Blower' car. Turner dramatically won again at the Whit Monday event with former Birkin mechanic Bill Rockell as his passenger. Devon landowner Richard Marker had bought another famed 4½-litre, 'Mother Gun', which he first entered for the MCC Sporting Trial in 1932, a feat that author David Venables reckons must have been the only time a Le Mans winner took home a reliability trial award. Then, over the Easter weekend, while Turner was winning at Brooklands, Marker took a silver award at the MCC Land's End Trial. Marker then made his Brooklands debut in the car at the August Bank Holiday meeting, winning the Byfleet Lighting Long Handicap. He also set the best time in a one-hour high-speed trial at the MCC members' day in September.

The following year 'Mother Gun' appeared with a single-seater body that had previously

been used by Dudley Froy for record breaking. It was not the only 4½-litre to appear at Brooklands that year, since in September Turner gave his former Paget No 3 'Blower' its final Brooklands outing. Marker continued to race 'Mother Gun', which was fitted with a 6½-litre engine and then, for 1937, was rebuilt by R.R. Jackson, given a new, aluminium single-seater body and renamed the Bentley-Jackson. It could still be a winner, taking the seven-lap Gold Star Handicap at the Whitsun meeting. It seemed a long time since 4½-litre Bentleys had competed in long-distance races but that year a standard Vanden Plas-bodied one was driven in a 12-hour sports car scratch race at Donington, driven by R. Wilcox and D.M. Steele. That the glory days were firmly over can be seen in its 23rd overall place. It was also second in the 5-litre class – for which there were two starters.

The 4½-litres continued to race at Brooklands, although a proposed ban at the track for cars over ten years old would have been the writing on the wall for its career had it not been for the Second World War, a couple appearing in the lists for the final,

somewhat surreal meeting held there in August 1939. One of them was that of Frank Elgood, a regular at Brooklands during those final years, who had been lauded in 1938 for memorably averaging 110.3mph during the MCC High Speed Trials there. That a model which came to be known for its racing had its origins in a road car could be seen in the fact that Elgood's car had started life as a 4½-litre saloon, although its chassis frame had now been shortened and a 2/4-seater body fitted.

ABOVE **Bentley 4½-litre models were on the grid for the first race ever organised by the Bentley Drivers Club, a two-lap handicap affair at Brooklands in 1936.** (W.O. Bentley Memorial Foundation)

LICENSED TO RACE

James Bond's creator, Ian Fleming, seems to have known his motor racing. In *Moonraker* we are told that 007 'once dabbled on the fringe of the racing world' and, pre-war, watched 'the Silver Arrows' compete at Tripoli and Berne. Fleming also left the outline for a motor racing story that Anthony Horowitz adapted for his own (2015) Bond novel *Trigger Mortis*. Horowitz admits that it was his own idea to place Bond in a Maserati 250F, but the car with which we must associate the hero is a blown Bentley 4½-litre. It is a car to which we are first introduced in *Casino Royale* as Bond's 'only personal hobby'. A 'battleship-grey convertible coupe', it is 'one of the last 4½-litres with the supercharger by Amherst Villiers'.

In a 1964 interview in *Playboy*, Fleming said: 'I probably chose the supercharged Bentley because Amherst Villiers was a great friend of mine and I knew something about it from my friendship with him.' Fleming had first met Villiers at an Oxford ball in 1927 and would, much later in their lives, paint a portrait of the author that was used in a special edition of *On Her Majesty's Secret Service*. It is no coincidence that the writers of the 2006 Bond movie *Casino Royale* chose the name 'Villiers' for one of M's staff.

In *Moonraker*, Fleming almost certainly evokes the 1930 Le Mans race as 007's Bentley chases the Mercedes Type 300S of villain Hugo Drax through Kent. 'Using the road as if it was Donington, Bond rammed his foot down and kept it there. Gradually, with the needle twitching either side of the hundred mark he began to narrow that gap.'

Forget the Aston Martins of the films; James Bond's car of choice is a supercharged Bentley 4½-litre.

Chapter Two

Anatomy of the Bentley 4½-litre

The Bentley 4½-litres were essentially hand-made cars with bodywork that would be sourced separately from outside companies. Thus, no two examples are exactly alike. Even the racing versions, albeit often entered by the factory, were privately owned and could, therefore, differ in specification. Leading racing car engineer Andy Brown here examines the basic make-up of both the unblown and the supercharged versions.

OPPOSITE 'I think the Bentleys are very nice to work on, very simple, very basic but way ahead of their time.' – Colin Smyrk, mechanic, NDR Ltd. *(Ian Wagstaff)*

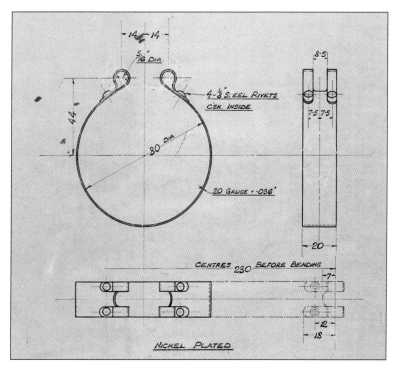

The first 4½-litre Bentley (a development of the earlier 3-litre) ran in the spring of 1927 and was used at Le Mans that year. The first production car then appeared in August 1927. Production ended in the summer of 1931, the car – and, indeed, almost Bentley as a company – being killed off by the stock market crash of October 1930.

No apology is made for the mixture of metric and imperial dimensions that follows – the Bentley drawings of the day contained this combination of dimensions. However, one common theme that came to light in researching the anatomy of the Bentley 4½-litre cars is how racing was used to improve the breed. A great many of the improvements made to the car during its production run were first tried on the race cars, primarily at Le Mans.

As all the cars were basically hand-made, and constant development took place on the production line, no two of the 4½-litre Bentleys are exactly alike.

Chassis

The type of construction used is that of a ladder-frame chassis – it is easy to see why it is called this when the bare frame is viewed. For the first of the 4½-litre cars, 0.156in (5/32in) thick steel was employed to form two substantial side beams and four sturdy cross-members. The chassis material thickness was increased to 0.188in (3/16in) thick for 1929 following failures experienced at Le Mans in 1928.

The side beams were also joined by tubular tie rods at the extreme front and rear. (In the 'Blower' version the front tie rod was split by the supercharger.) Beam stiffness was increased on the long wheelbase cars by the fitment of

FAR LEFT The front 'dumb iron' is what defines the chassis number. *(Andy Brown)*

LEFT Cross-member at the rear of the chassis. *(Andy Brown)*

BELOW Locomotive-type chassis-stiffening strut gear. *(Andy Brown)*

locomotive-style struts under the side rails, most likely a result of W.O. Bentley's engineering apprenticeship with the Great Northern Railway.

Engine

This was first run on the test bench in February 1927. The design was somewhat of a hybrid between the earlier four-cylinder 3-litre and the six-cylinder 6½-litre. It was an efficient cross-flow design, the fuel mixture inlets being on the right-hand side of the block and the exhaust outlets on the left-hand side.

With the bottom end being almost identical to the 3-litre, it also had the same cylinder spacing as the smaller engine, but with the bore (100mm) and stroke (140mm) of the 6½-litre (hence the swept volume was actually 4.4 litres despite always being referred to as 4½ – and the bigger engine is 6.6 litres, not 6½…).

Initially built with a compression ratio of 4.8:1, rated at 110bhp, revised pistons were fitted in March/April 1928, which raised the compression ratio to 5.3:1. For racing purposes this was raised to 6.0:1 (125bhp @ 3,500rpm) by machining the crankcase and block and fitting high-compression pistons. For the Le Mans team the compression ratio was raised still further to 6.12:1, giving 130bhp @ 3,500rpm.

The exhaust manifold casting looks massive

ABOVE Strut gear mounting points. *(Ian Wagstaff)*

LEFT Engine block/head casting. *(Ian Wagstaff)*

Bentley 4½-litre 'Blower'.

(Tony Matthews)

1 Fuel filler cap
2 Fuel tank
3 Folding hood
4 Rear-view mirror
5 Fuel-tank pressure hand pump
6 Wire-mesh windscreen
   (folded down)
7 Dynamo flexible drive
8 Spare spark plug storage
9 Boost blow-off valves
10 4½-litre engine
11 Inlet manifold
12 Leather bonnet strap
13 Radiator water cap
14 SU carburettors
15 Wire-mesh carburettor guard
16 Supercharger
17 Horn
18 Front friction damper
19 Front brake drum
20 Worm and wheel steering box
21 Steering linkage
22 Steering column
23 Flywheel ring gear
24 Front brake actuating rod
25 Clutch
26 Gearbox
27 Locomotive-type chassis
   stiffening gear
28 Gearchange lever
29 Handbrake
30 Handbrake linkage
31 Propeller shaft
32 Ladder-frame chassis
33 Rear leaf spring
34 Differential housing
35 Rear friction damper
36 Rear brake drum
37 Double-eared wheel locknut
38 Dunlop 6.75/7.00 x 21 tyre

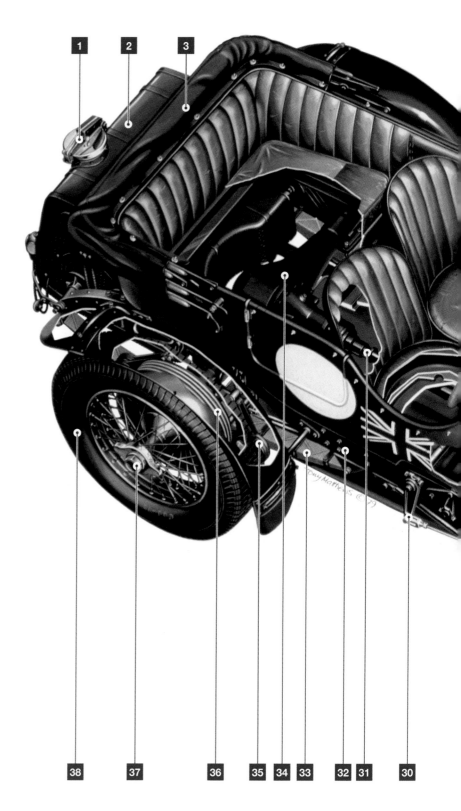

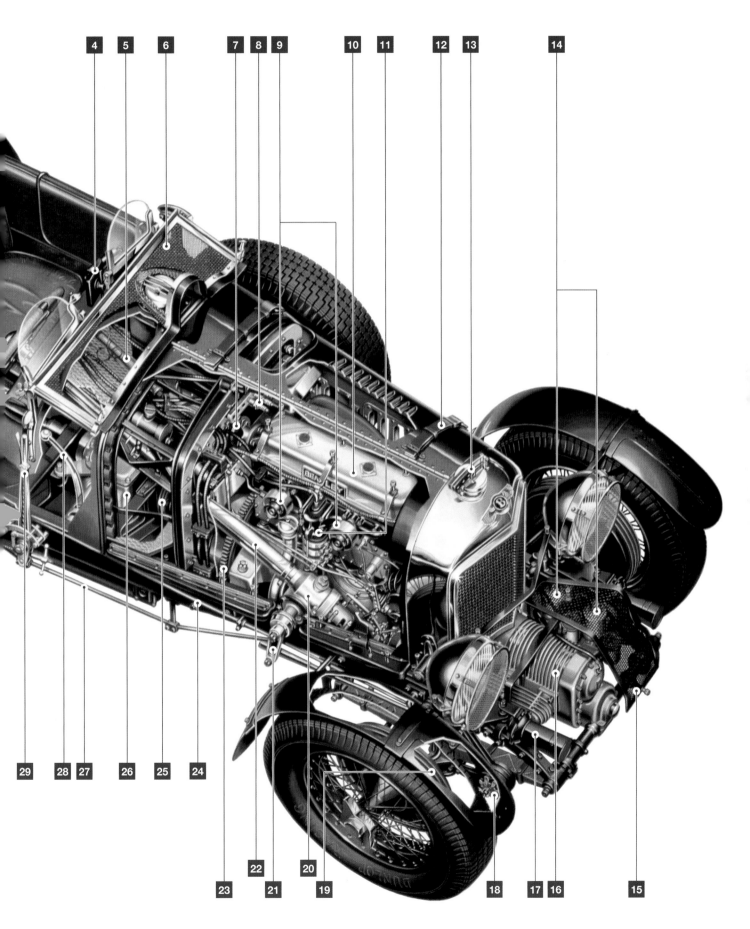

45

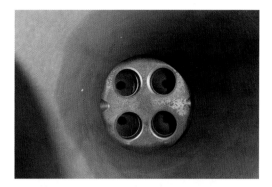

RIGHT Internal view of an engine cylinder showing the inlet and exhaust ports, and also the threaded holes for the two spark plugs. *(Ian Wagstaff)*

FAR RIGHT The camshaft showing three lobes per cylinder and the spiral drive gear. *(Andy Brown)*

RIGHT Valves and valve guide. *(Andy Brown)*

by modern standards, but the consequent volume promoted good gas flow that aided the engine efficiency.

A rev limit of 3,500rpm was recommended – if run at 4,000+, the BDC handbook on the Vintage Bentley states, 'Renew block, pistons, crankcase, con rods and start again!'

Block

The block and heads were cast as one component, a more reliable arrangement than having separate block and cylinder head (as anyone who has encountered a leaking head gasket can testify) but a more difficult prospect for the machine shop. Each cylinder had

RIGHT The heavy crankshaft of the supercharged engine. *(Andy Brown)*

RIGHT A modern counter-balanced replacement crank for the supercharged engine. *(Andy Brown)*

two inlet and two exhaust valves, which was unusual for the day as most engines of the period only had one inlet and/or one exhaust valve. This also contributed to the efficient airflow through the engine. The block was also machined to take two spark plugs per cylinder. To increase reliability, W.O. Bentley built a level of 'redundancy' into his cars; two spark plugs improved the flame burn of the inlet charge, improving horsepower, while an added advantage was that in a situation where a spark plug (or even one magneto) failed, the engine would continue to run – albeit at reduced performance.

A 'heavy crank block' replaced the original casting in the supercharged engines, this being necessary to match the increased main bearing stud spacing to suit the bigger diameter bearings of the heavy crank needed in the Blower engines. It was also fitted to 'heavy crank' unblown engines from about February 1930. (To reduce production costs, a degree of component commonality was adopted later in the production run.)

Camshaft

The single camshaft was positioned along the top of the block between the two rows of valves, supported by five white metal bearings. It was driven from the crankshaft via a vertical driveshaft on the front of the engine, and a top and bottom pair of spiral bevel gear assemblies (see 'Ignition system' on page 53 for details of the bottom bevel gear). There were three cam lobes per cylinder, two operating the exhaust valves via a pair of rockers, and one lobe for the two inlet valves via a single forked rocker. Rockers that were originally of steel for the 3-litre were manufactured from duralumin for the 4.5-litre. Hardened steel rollers on the inboard end of the rockers followed the cam lobes. Ball-ended tappets on the outboard end of the rockers actuated the valves.

Crankshaft

Five white metal bearings supported the crankshaft, with a double-ball thrust bearing forward of the front main bearing to prevent end float and oppose the clutch disengagement forces.

LEFT Standard (vertical) and heavy (horizontal) crank case castings. *(Andy Brown)*

A heavy-type crank (weighing 72lb) replaced the original crank (47lb) to cope with the increased demands of the supercharged engines that were first produced in early 1930. The designer of the supercharger, Amherst Villiers, had recommended a counter-balanced crankshaft, but W.O. Bentley felt that just increasing the size (and weight) would be sufficient. In retrospect a counterbalanced crank would have been preferable, as the heavy crank promoted an out of balance vibration leading to failures of the middle main bearing when the cars were pushed to the limit. Hence a modern after-market crank has been made available for current owners of the supercharged cars.

The size of the engine main bearings was also increased (from 55 to 80mm) to cope with the increase in weight of the crank, requiring modified crankcases. To standardise the components required for the entire range and keep costs down (which was important following the stock market crash of late 1929), the heavy crank (albeit with the spigot for the supercharger drive cut off) and modified crankcase were then also fitted to unblown engines from late 1930. The increased weight

RIGHT Con rod.
(Ian Wagstaff)

did reduce performance, but the engine consequently ran more smoothly.

Con rods

These were designed with 290mm centres (reduced to 285mm for the supercharged cars because of bigger diameter gudgeon pins being fitted – 25mm as opposed to the original 20mm – to cope with the increased loads), with a web thickness of 1.75mm and a flange thickness of 2.25mm.

In March 1928 the original floating-type gudgeon pins were replaced with pins held in place by circlips, but the new design was soon abandoned as the circlips were found to work loose and score the cylinder bores.

In May 1929 steel shell big end bearings lined with white metal replaced the earlier 'direct-metalled' white metal bearings. This change was made for reliability reasons, as the bearing material was prone to cracking in service on the initial con rods. This entailed enlarging the big end bore diameter from 57 to 61mm.

Throttle linkage

The throttle butterflies on the carburettors could be actuated either by a lever on the steering column boss – although this was less likely to be found on the racing cars – or by foot pedal (see 'Interior' section).

The hand-lever linkage actuated a vertical rod forward of the carburettors. This rod comprised a small diameter top section that could slide within the larger diameter lower section. The amount that the top inner rod could drop back into the lower tube was set by the position of a pinch clamp on the top shaft. The hand lever could thereby be used to set a minimum throttle opening (say to maintain a high idle speed, over 1,000rpm being needed to stop the spark plugs of the supercharged engine from fouling). When the foot pedal was depressed, calling for more open butterflies via a separate linkage, the top inner rod would slide out of the larger diameter lower rod.

ABOVE Two of the various Bentley piston designs (split skirt and additional piston (oil wiper) ring) – note crowned top. *(Andy Brown)*

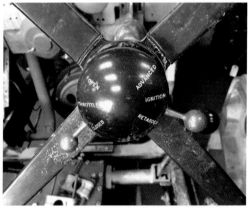

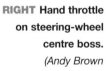

RIGHT Hand throttle on steering-wheel centre boss. *(Andy Brown*

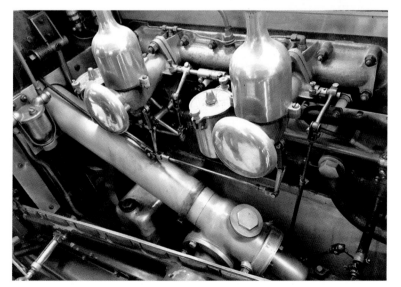

LEFT Throttle linkage – hand throttle shaft/tube and pinch clamp can be seen just to the right of the right-hand (forward) carburettor. *(Author)*

Fuel system

The initial fuel tank of 16 gallons was mounted at the extreme rear of the chassis. The 1927 and 1928 'touring' bodywork style Le Mans cars were fitted with 30-gallon fuel tanks, giving them a duration of around three hours between fuel stops. The 'bobtail' rear bodywork introduced in 1928 resulted in a reduction in fuel tank capacity to 25 gallons.

On YW 5758, one of the 1929 Le Mans team cars, the rear of the exhaust pipe runs in a small channel in the underside of the fuel tank. The theory behind this was that the heat from the exhaust would slightly pressurise the tank and help provide positive fuel pressure (this before the days when the benefits of lowering the temperature of the fuel inlet charge were appreciated).

Initial pressure was provided via a pump handle mounted on the dash (see 'Dash' section); a pressure of 2.5psi would be enough to start the car.

On production cars, an 'Autovac' unit was fitted on the front face of the bulkhead. This was effectively the fuel pump, and comprised two hollow chambers. For the 4½-litre cars the bottom chamber took the form of a cylindrical tank, mounted horizontally with the axis running fore and aft through the dash bulkhead. This tank was of half-a-gallon capacity, was open to the atmosphere and formed the reservoir tank from which the carburettors were fed via gravity. The top chamber (a vertically orientated cylinder, 'teed' into the bottom tank) was separated from the bottom tank via a drop valve.

The top chamber was connected via a pipe to a fitting on the inlet manifold between the two carburettors. When the engine was running, the low pressure in the inlet manifold thus created a partial vacuum in the top chamber of the Autovac. This low pressure would draw up the drop valve connecting the two chambers, and thus a low pressure in the top chamber would be formed. This would then pull fuel from the tank at the rear of the car into the top chamber (passing through a fuel filter mounted on the extreme right of the front face of the bulkhead). As the fuel level rose in the top chamber, a float would also rise, and when this reached a certain level two valves would be actuated. One would blank off the suction pipe from

RIGHT Autovac (fuel pump) unit – note spare spark plug storage on top of distributor drive cover.
(Andy Brown)

RIGHT AND FAR RIGHT Fuel-tank air pressure and fuel lines.
(Andy Brown)

the inlet manifold. The other would open the top chamber to the atmosphere, which would allow the fuel it contained to drop into the lower chamber. The float thus dropping in the upper chamber would close the valve to the atmosphere and open the valve to the suction pipe, and the process of pulling fuel from the main fuel tank would begin again.

However, this process was not always sufficient to keep the lower tank from running dry, especially under prolonged running at full throttle. Hence the process was augmented by the exhaust heat generating positive pressure in the rear tank, and why for most race car fuel systems (and for all the supercharged cars)

the Autovac was replaced by electric pumps. Should the lower tank of the Autovac run dry, it could be filled directly from the filler neck on the right-hand side of the unit.

Of the four lines running from the top of the fuel tank, isolated by 'taps', the left-hand two were for 'air pressure in' (connected to the pump on the dash) and to release the air pressure from the tank (it was necessary to do this when switching off the engine). The right-hand taps allowed the fuel to flow from either the main or the reserve fuel tanks.

The initial cars proved difficult to start, so in February 1928 a Ki-gas injector was fitted. This was in effect a primer pump, operated via a knob on the dash that injected neat fuel into the cylinders during the starting process.

Because of the increased demand of the supercharged engines, twin 'Autopulse' electric pumps were fitted, while a 25-gallon fuel tank was fitted to the road car version.

Carburettors

The carburettors were mounted on an inlet manifold on the right-hand side of the engine. The cars were initially fitted with twin SU G5 'sloper' carburettors, replaced on production cars in 1929 by vertically mounted SU HG5 units, which had first been tried at Le Mans in 1928. A

BELOW Original 'sloper' carburettors.
(Andy Brown)

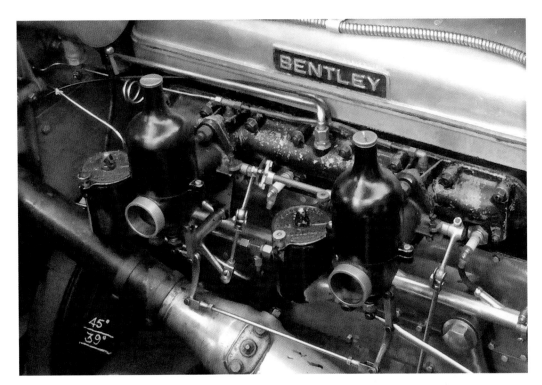

major difference with these was that the throttle butterflies were now part of the carburettor body and not fitted in the inlet manifold as with the 'slopers'. The later carburettors were also fitted with flame dampers to protect the inside of the bonnet from 'backfires' through the carburettors.

On the supercharged cars, two carburettors were mounted on the left-hand side of the supercharger forward of the car's radiator. These were therefore protected by a wire mesh guard.

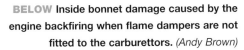

RIGHT Supercharger on the bench at NDR with carburettors removed, and showing the top rotor drive gears. (Andy Brown)

RIGHT Supercharger outlet manifold. (Andy Brownr)

BELOW Supercharged engine showing the pressure blow-off valves. (Ian Wagstaff)

Supercharger

Manufactured by Amherst Villiers, this was of a twin-rotor 'Roots' type and was constantly engaged. The decision to mount the supercharger on the front of the engine, therefore extending forward beyond the radiator (and thus becoming an instantly recognisable feature of the car), came about because of W.O. Bentley's aversion to using chains or belts to drive ancillary components. This was due to his conviction that these forms of drive were less reliable than direct drive or gears. (Hence the gear-driven vertical shaft on the front of the engine to drive the magnetos, water pump and camshaft.)

The input to the supercharger was therefore taken directly from the front of the revised ('heavy') crank, via a fabric UJ, driving the bottom rotor at engine speed. The top rotor was then driven via a pair of gears at the rear of the supercharger.

The carburettors were mounted on the left-hand side of the supercharger as described above. A cast manifold on the right-hand side of the turbocharger (with a significant number of fins incorporated in the casting to increase stiffness and to help cool the inlet charge) fed the compressed air/fuel mixture to the rear of the supercharger, where it was connected to a 90° pipe that took the mixture up to the inlet manifold. To prevent damage to the supercharger from the engine backfiring, two blow-off valves were incorporated into the inlet manifold on the right-hand side of the engine and (on production cars) a third valve fitted on the underside of the exhaust manifold.

The first design of supercharger comprised two rotors, fitted inside a casing with a smooth outer surface and double-walled in places. However, as the supercharger became hot the casing was found to expand at different rates, owing to the different wall thicknesses, and the subsequent distortion would cause contact with the rotors. The casing was therefore redesigned with a single wall (to eliminate the differential expansion), the exterior now being cast with a significant number of fins/ribs for cooling and increased stiffness.

The supercharger certainly worked as intended, the engine producing 240bhp at 4,200rpm (delivering an inlet charge at 10–11psi relative pressure) compared to the 130bhp (at

3,500rpm) of the unblown engine in Le Mans trim. Even in road car format the power output was raised from 110bhp to 175bhp (at an inlet charge relative pressure of 9.5–10psi). This was not without a downside, however, engine reliability being seriously affected.

Ignition system

Twin magnetos were used, initially ML GR4 but replaced by the more powerful ER4 in February 1928 to reduce the drain on the battery during engine starting. There was one magneto on each side of the engine, each firing the four spark plugs on either side, *ie* there were two spark plugs per cylinder, one on each side of the block. The magnetos were set up to fire both plugs per cylinder simultaneously, to provide the biggest ignition spark possible. If one magneto failed only one plug per cylinder would fire, but the engine would still run. The magnetos were fitted to a 'turret' mounted on the front of the top of the crankcase, and were driven via a bevel gear on the front of the crankshaft, through a vertical shaft running up

LEFT Early supercharger casing. *(Andy Brown)*

LEFT Magnetos either side of the front of the engine. *(Andy Brown)*

FAR LEFT Magneto/ water pump turret. *(Andy Brown)*

LEFT Magneto drive cross-shaft. *(Andy Brown)*

FAR LEFT Magneto mounting flange showing the stack of spring steel plates used to drive the magneto. *(Andy Brown)*

LEFT Ignition timing control on the steering wheel boss. *(Andy Brown)*

RIGHT AND FAR RIGHT Ignition timing linkage in advanced and retarded positions. *(Andy Brown)*

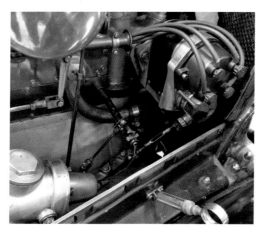

the front of the engine to a cross-shaft driven by a worm gear connected to the vertical driveshaft at the top of the turret. The magnetos were directly driven by a stack of spring steel plates, fixed in each end of the cross-shaft. These reduced shock loading on the magnetos and protected them from vibration.

To aid engine starting, the spark timing could be adjusted via a lever on the steering wheel centre boss that was connected via a mechanical linkage to the magnetos.

The supercharged cars were fitted with Bosch FF4 or FV4B magnetos. In all cases the contact breaker gap was recommended as 0.012in, the spark plug gap being set at 0.018in to 0.019in.

Electrical system

A double pole (not earthed, but a continuous wiring loop) electrical system, manufactured by Smiths, was fitted for lighting and starting. With the magneto ignition system and the air-pressure driven fuel system, an electrical system was not required once the engine was running; in theory the engine could be started via a crank handle, so that the electrical system was in principle not required at all for engine running.

The 12V battery was charged by a dynamo

BELOW Initial electrical system – double pole. *(W.O. Bentley Memorial Foundation)*

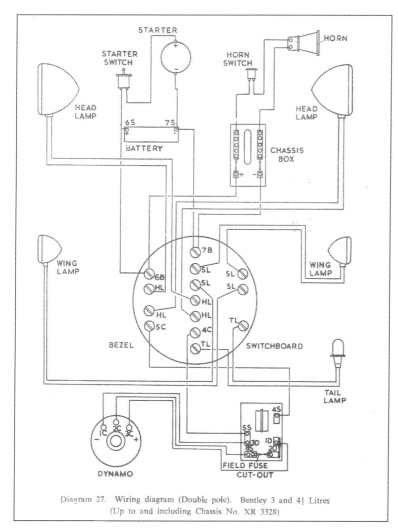

Diagram 27. Wiring diagram (Double pole). Bentley 3 and 4½ Litres (Up to and including Chassis No. XR 3328)

BELOW Dynamo. *(Andy Brown)*

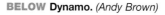

(Smiths 2DA–12A) mounted on the bulkhead behind the engine, driven directly from the rear end of the camshaft via fabric universal joints.

An early form of regulator was employed which automatically connected the dynamo to the battery once it was turning fast enough to generate a charge, and to also disconnect it when the dynamo rpm dropped below charging level (so that the battery did not discharge back through the dynamo). However, to prevent the battery from overcharging on long runs the driver had to manually disconnect the dynamo from the battery using a switch on the dashboard.

The system was upgraded to a single pole (earthed) fused system (still made by Smiths) for 1929. The fuse box was placed on the front of the bulkhead, to the left-hand side of the engine.

Starter motor

The Smiths Type 4 LSA starter motor was mounted low down at the rear of the left-hand side of the engine in a housing that was part

BELOW Starter motor (and oil filler). *(Andy Brown)*

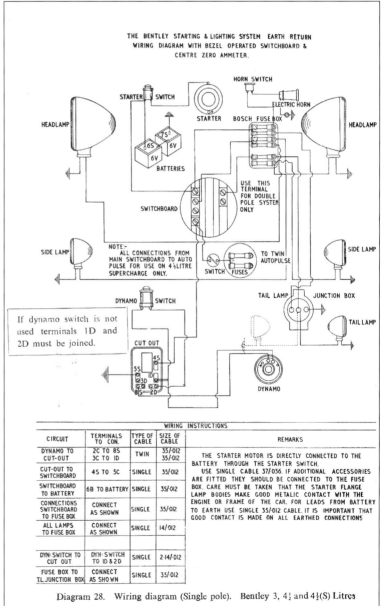

THE BENTLEY STARTING & LIGHTING SYSTEM EARTH RETURN WIRING DIAGRAM WITH BEZEL OPERATED SWITCHBOARD & CENTRE ZERO AMMETER.

WIRING INSTRUCTIONS				
CIRCUIT	TERMINALS TO CON.	TYPE OF CABLE	SIZE OF CABLE	REMARKS
DYNAMO TO CUT-OUT	2C TO 8S 3C TO 1D	TWIN	35/.012 35/.012	THE STARTER MOTOR IS DIRECTLY CONNECTED TO THE BATTERY THROUGH THE STARTER SWITCH. USE SINGLE CABLE 37/.036. IF ADDITIONAL ACCESSORIES ARE FITTED THEY SHOULD BE CONNECTED TO THE FUSE BOX. CARE MUST BE TAKEN THAT THE STARTER FLANGE LAMP BODIES MAKE GOOD METALIC CONTACT WITH THE ENGINE OR FRAME OF THE CAR. FOR LEADS FROM BATTERY TO EARTH USE SINGLE 35/.012 CABLE. IT IS IMPORTANT THAT GOOD CONTACT IS MADE ON ALL EARTHED CONNECTIONS
CUT-OUT TO SWITCHBOARD	4S TO 5C	SINGLE	35/.012	
SWITCHBOARD TO BATTERY	6B TO BATTERY	SINGLE	35/.012	
CONNECTIONS SWITCHBOARD TO FUSE BOX	CONNECT AS SHOWN	SINGLE	35/.012	
ALL LAMPS TO FUSE BOX	CONNECT AS SHOWN	SINGLE	14/.012	
DYN. SWITCH TO CUT OUT	DYN. SWITCH TO 1D & 2D	SINGLE	2.14/.012	
FUSE BOX TO TL. JUNCTION BOX	CONNECT AS SHOWN	SINGLE	35/.012	

Diagram 28. Wiring diagram (Single pole). Bentley 3, 4½ and 4½(S) Litres (From and including 4½ Chassis No. XR 3329)

of the crankcase casting. It drove a ring gear shrink-fitted around the engine flywheel via a Bendix automatic pinion.

Lighting

One of the most characteristic features of the Bentley was its two large headlights situated one either side of the radiator grille. The size of the reflectors was necessary to amplify the poor luminescence of the light bulbs of the day, but even so, Neil Davis of NDR Ltd still refers to them as 'Dim and Dimmer'! They were protected by substantial mesh guards, although this did detract from the level of illumination.

BELOW **Headlights, additional horn and dampers on Bentley Team Car.** (Andy Brown)

YW 5758

Consequently for Le Mans in 1928 a third, even larger diameter headlight was fitted, although this affected engine cooling by blocking the airflow to the radiator and was not seen in future events.

Horns

The horns were retained on the race cars, as many races, including Le Mans, were held on public roads with near non-existent crowd control. Additional (larger/louder) horns were fitted to the running boards between the mudguards on some of the Le Mans cars. They were electrically operated by a switch on the dashboard.

Cooling system

An aluminium-bodied water pump was mounted on the front of the magneto turret at the front of the engine. This fed the coolant into the lower front of the right-hand water-jacket plate. The water then exited the block via five outlets just above the exhaust manifold, which were connected via a water pipe; a thermostat was mounted on the front of this pipe from the 45th chassis onwards, as the initial cars were overcooled. A hose from the upswept pipe at the outlet of the thermostat took the water back to the radiator.

The water radiator shell was manufactured from nickel silver, and a header tank on top of the radiator made for a very tall unit, which gave the car its characteristic straight-top bonnet line. For speed of topping up the water system on the race cars a large filler cap with a quick-release over-centre locking lever was fitted.

In anticipation of the increased cooling requirements of the bigger 4½-litre engine, as well as being built with a larger radiator than the preceding 3-litre car (giving a total water capacity of 5¾ gallons), a cooling fan was initially fitted. In practice, it was found that the engine was overcooled and the fan was omitted. The main problem with the pulley-and-belt-driven fan was that when it was really needed – *ie* at low engine rpm when running at low speed in traffic – the fan would turn over slowly and not be of much help in increasing the airflow through the radiator. But when running at high speeds, when there was already a relatively high volume of cooling air passing

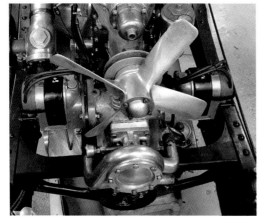

through the radiator due to the forward motion
of the car, the fan would also be turning at high
speed, when it was not required.

There was a further reliability concern in
that the fans were quite substantial castings
– almost works of art in themselves, not the
lightweight pressings or plastic mouldings of
today – and if a blade was to break off (due
possibly to an occlusion in the casting) the
amount of damage that this could cause, plus
the resultant amount of vibration, would have
been substantial. In addition, because of the
overcooling issues, a thermostat was fitted from
the 45th car onwards.

Cooling could be adversely affected by a
build-up of sludge in the water system. This
was found to be aluminium residue due to
corrosion of the water-pump body and the
water-jacket plates on the side of the block.
In 1929, therefore, the material used in the
manufacture of the water-pump body was
changed to a more corrosion-resistant type,
and stainless steel ('Staybright' in its day) was
used for the water-jacket plates.

Whereas the unblown 4½-litre cars had been
overcooled, the supercharged cars suffered
from the opposite issue. The bottom of the
radiator had to be removed to accommodate
the supercharger, and so, even though the core
was increased in thickness to try to compensate
for this, the supercharged engine cooling system
only held 5 gallons as opposed to the 5¾ gallons
of the unblown engine. The supercharger also
blocked airflow over the oil sump which then
increased the oil temperature, and hence the
overall temperature of the engine, meaning that a
further increase in water cooling was required.

No separate oil cooler was fitted; the sump

was arranged such that it sat below the chassis
in the airflow under the car. The race cars had
a much larger volume sump (the increased oil
quantity helping the cooling by reducing the
duty cycle of the oil), and the larger volume
casting also incorporated fins cast into the sides
to further enhance the oil cooling.

ABOVE Water jacket
plates on the ends
and sides of the block.
(Andy Brown)

Oil system

The engine sump was a one-piece
magnesium casting. The Birkin (racing) sump
was cast with transverse baffles (sited between
the lobes of the crankshaft) to oppose oil surge
under braking and acceleration. The oil pump, of
a gear-wheel type, was mounted at the front of
the bottom of the sump, and was driven by the
bevel gear on the front of the crank. The pump
fed oil through the filter (also in the crankcase) to
distribution pipes for the camshaft, etc.

Changes to the lubrication system as the
car was developed, mainly due to competition
experience, included improving the oil supply to

ABOVE LEFT Standard sump. *(Andy Brown)*

ABOVE CENTRE Increased capacity Birkin (racing) sump with cooling fins added. *(Andy Brown)*

ABOVE RIGHT Internal view of the Birkin sump showing the transverse baffles. *(Andy Brown)*

BELOW Exhaust manifold drawing. *(W.O. Bentley Memorial Foundation)*

the con rod bottom end bearings at the same time as the separate coated steel shell bearings were introduced, and a redesign of the rocker casings to create an oil bath for the rocker rollers.

On the supercharged cars oil was supplied to the supercharger via a gravity feed from the cam casing. A pump was used to scavenge excess oil from the supercharger and return it to the engine sump.

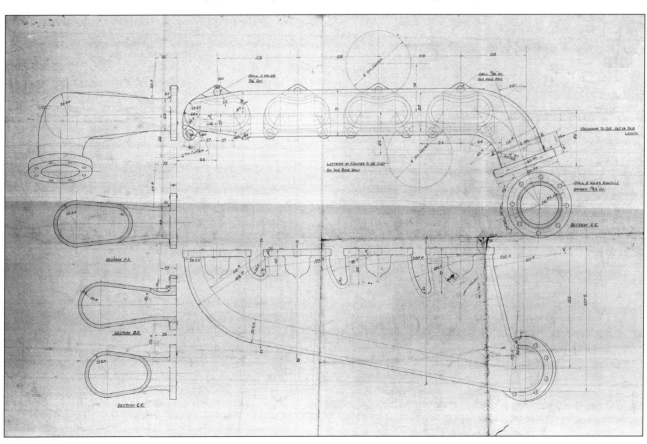

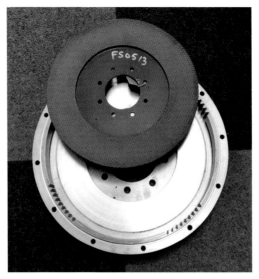

Exhaust

The exhaust system was a 'four-into-one'
manifold casting, the large dimensions
of which helped with engine breathing. The
downpipe from the exhaust manifold was clad
with asbestos kept in place with ¼in mesh wire
netting to form a heat shield.

A 'pepper pot' silencer was initially fitted, but
a Pulswell silencer was fitted in 1930 primarily
to closed-body cars to help reduce the 'engine
thumping' experienced by passengers. This was
adopted on all models to streamline production of
the range and hence reduce costs.

Transmission

Clutch

The clutch was initially a cone type with
Ferodo lining. The large-diameter outer
section was bolted to the engine flywheel. The
smaller diameter centre section was kept in
contact with the outer section via a coil spring
fitted to the centre of the assembly. As the
clutch pedal was depressed, conical rollers
either side of the clutch output shaft were
brought into contact with the boss at the rear
of the conical centre section of the clutch and
pushed it forward out of contact with the outer
cone, thus disconnecting the engine drive from
the gearbox output shaft.

To help with matching the gearbox input and
output shaft speeds during shifting, the input
shaft could be fitted with a brake disc. As the
clutch pedal was depressed this then brought a

friction pad (mounted on a spring steel plate to
the rear of this brake disc) into contact with the
disc to reduce the rpm of the gearbox input shaft.

The cone-type clutch was replaced with a
more modern plate type in 1929 (this having
been run on team cars at Le Mans in 1928).

Gearbox

The gearbox contained four forward gears and
one reverse gear. Synchromesh had yet to be
invented, hence this was a 'crash' gearbox
which involved the driver double-declutching
so as not to graunch the gears. (See also the
'Clutch' section above.)

It was mounted on three points on the chassis
frame, the front being adjustable in height for
shaft alignment purposes. Note that the gearbox

was not mounted directly to the engine as on
most modern cars. This helped with accessibility
and ease of servicing. Any misalignment of the
crank and gearbox shafts (inevitable, as the
ladder chassis had all the torsional stiffness of
a wet noodle) was corrected for either by fabric
disc universal joints (see just forward of the
input shaft brake disc in the photos in the clutch
section) or by a cleverly machined set of teeth on
the front end of the shaft that fitted into the centre
of the clutch cone. This was machined to have
radii on both the sides and the top of the teeth
that fitted into the internal spline of the clutch and
allowed up to 15° of misalignment.

The initial cars were fitted with the Bentley
'C-Type' gearbox (the 'A' and 'B' types being
fitted to the 3-litre), but this was replaced by the
'D-Type' in March 1928. The revised gearbox
had closer ratios, with a taller third to provide
the driver with 'sportier' performance than was
available from the more widely spaced top
gears in the C-Type. The D-Type ratios were

the same as those in the A-Type gearbox in
the 3-litre car (but note the longer final drive
in the 4½-litre car that gave it a higher road
speed in each gear), but the 'D' gearbox was
also redesigned to cope with the greater torque
of the 4½-litre. Amongst the improvements
learned over eight years of development that
were incorporated into the 'D' were:

■ The main and lay shafts were reduced
   in length to reduce distortion under the
   increased loads. The shafts were also multi-
   splined to better cope with the loads.
■ Whilst the speedometer drive was still on the
   left-hand side, it was completely redesigned
   from the C-Type gearbox.
■ The D-Type gate had increased dimensions
   (3 x 4¾in as opposed to the 2¾ x 2¼in
   for the C-Type) to make it less likely for the
   driver to select the wrong gear. (Note in the
   'Interior' section photos for the relatively
   poor accessibility of the gear lever, low down
   beside the driver's right knee.)
■ The oil filler was now fitted low on the left-
   hand side.

The D-type box can also be recognised by its
domed top plate with inset brass vent.

In both types of gearbox the input and
output shafts were inline, the lay shaft being
offset low on the left. In both 'boxes, top gear
was direct drive, third gear sliding over fourth to
lock the input and output shaft together – ie so

RIGHT Gear cluster in
neutral. (Andy Brown)

FAR RIGHT Gear
cluster with 'direct
drive' top (fourth)
gear engaged. Note
relationship of top two
gears compared to
when in neutral.
(Andy Brown)

that the propshaft rpm then matched that of the engine crankshaft.

A reverse idler was fitted low down on the left side of the gearbox giving the same ratio (road speed) as in first gear. A reverse lock-out was provided by a sprung loaded rod on the side of the gear lever, which had to be lifted via a hook at its top end to enable the gear lever to be moved over to the right and back to engage reverse.

Propshaft

The propshaft was initially fitted with a substantial universal joint to the rear of the gearbox, and with a sliding plunge joint (made up of phosphor bronze pads and sliding blocks) to the differential nosepiece. The plunge joint was needed to account for the necessity for the propshaft to change in length due to rear-axle vertical motion. The initial plunge joint was the same as fitted to the earlier 3-litre car, but due to excessive wear – possibly made worse by the increase in power output from the 4½-litre engine – this design was replaced (in 1928) with an off-the-shelf Hardy Spicer design, which incorporated enclosed splines and was supplied fully balanced.

Final drive

The final drive took the form of a spiral bevel gear and pinion, with a ratio of 3.533:1 for the road cars (considerably taller than the 4.23:1 of the 3-litre cars, indicating the anticipated increase in top speed). For racing at Le Mans an even taller final drive (3.333:1) was fitted. Yet taller final drives (3.0:1 and 2.8:1) were available for faster tracks (like Brooklands) and attempted record runs. These would also be used by the faster supercharged cars.

Differential

An open differential with four planet gears was employed on all the cars. The racing differentials were fitted with a carrier across the rear to stop the sides of the housing from spreading apart under load. They also had small scoops riveted to the planet gear carrier to scoop oil from the 'sump' of the outer casing into the centre of the

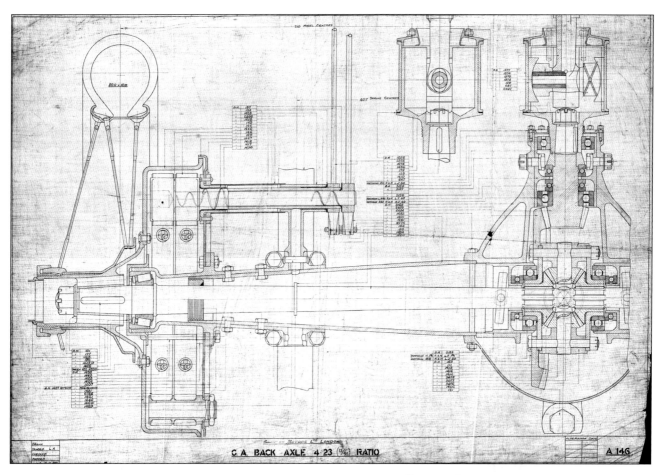

C.A. BACK AXLE 4·23 (¹³/₄₆) RATIO   A.146.

ABOVE General arrangement drawing of the rear axle. Note two sets of brake shoes per wheel, plunge joint between propshaft and differential nosepiece. *(W.O. Bentley Memorial Foundation)*

BELOW Rear axle. *(Andy Brown)*

differential; otherwise, owing to the centrifugal effect of the rotating assembly, the differential would have run dry due to the oil being thrown to the outside. A removable nosepiece connected the differential to the propshaft for ease of maintenance.

Driveshaft

The driveshafts ran inside the rear axle, having bearings at the outboard ends and being splined at the inboard ends to form a semi-floating arrangement.

Steering and suspension

As was common practice at the time, semi-elliptic leaf springs were fitted at each corner of the car. The front springs were mounted above the axle, the axle being of a simple beam type. At each end of the front beam was a boss that took a pivot pin, upon which the steering stub axles were mounted.

The wheel hubs rotated around the stub axles on two needle roller bearings, with excessive preload being prevented by machining the thickness of a 'security washer' on the end of the assembly so that it would bottom out on the end of the stub axle just before clamping the bearing tight (0.006in of clearance being recommended when cold). Then, with component expansion due to the heat generated when the car was running, this clearance all but disappeared. In this way the bearing end nut could be clamped up tight.

The driver's movement of the steering wheel was carried directly by a straight steering column to a worm and wheel steering box mounted low down on the chassis frame next

to the right-hand side of the engine. A lever arm dropped down from the steering box and was connected via a spring-loaded ball joint to a forward running rod that connected to a curved steering arm (via the same type of joint) on the right-hand stub axle.

The steering input was conveyed to the left-hand side via an adjustable track rod fitted between the stub axles (again with a spring-loaded ball joint at each end). The machining of left- and right-hand threads at either end of the track rod enabled relatively easy adjustment of the toe-in on the front wheels.

An early form of 'steering damper' involved replacing the original rigid-spoke steering wheel with a spring-spoke type manufactured by Bluemel. Although this improved the handling from the point of view of the driver it was not universally liked, as the spokes could break in an accident, when the resultant sharp edges and the relatively small-diameter steering wheel centre hub could cause serious chest injuries, whereas a solid-spoked steering

wheel spread the force of an impact over a much wider area.

The rear springs were mounted below the rear axle to better control the torque reaction from the engine. The rear axle had in its centre a 'banjo' casing for the differential, the casing being manufactured by Rubery Owen. Steel pressings fitted to either side of the differential casing carried the driveshafts.

The shock absorbers fitted were of friction damper type, basically a series of alternating

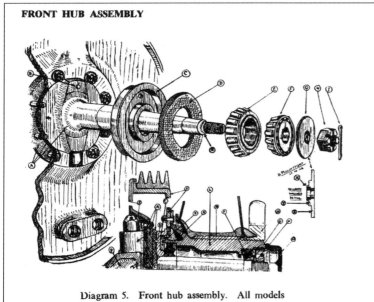

FRONT HUB ASSEMBLY

Diagram 5. Front hub assembly. All models

(A) Stub axle unit.
(B) Dust cap dowel pin.
(C) Inner dust cover.
(D) Felt washer.
(E) Inner roller race.
(F) Outer roller race.
(G) Security washer.
(H) ¼" BSF slotted nut.
(I) 5/32" split pin.
(X) Flange of security washer.
(Y) Stepped inner face of washer..
(Z) Remainder of face of washer.

ABOVE Front hub assembly. *(W.O. Bentley Memorial Foundation)*

RIGHT Steering linkage. *(Andy Brown)*

steel and oil-impregnated applewood discs operated by levers connected to the axles and the frame. The level of damping was adjusted by increasing or decreasing the clamping load across the friction discs, using a threaded nut wound down on to a star-shaped spring washer on the outside of the disc assembly.

RIGHT Late version Perrot shaft (with cover removed).
(Andy Brown)

The performance of these could be badly affected by dust and/or grit getting into the disc assemblies, a common problem due to the road conditions of the day.

The original DN dampers were replaced by Bentley & Draper units in 1928. Ride quality could also be tuned by adjusting the camber (amount of bend) in the leaf-spring assemblies.

Brakes

The brakes were relatively large diameter (by modern standards – 400mm) ribbed steel drums fitted front and rear, with aluminium brake shoes. The brakes could be actuated via a foot pedal and/or a hand lever, which was mounted on the outside of the bodywork on the right-hand side (although the hand lever only operated the rear brakes).

On the first of the 4½-litre cars driver actuation of the brakes was conveyed to the hubs via Perrot shafts that allowed for both steering and suspension vertical travel.

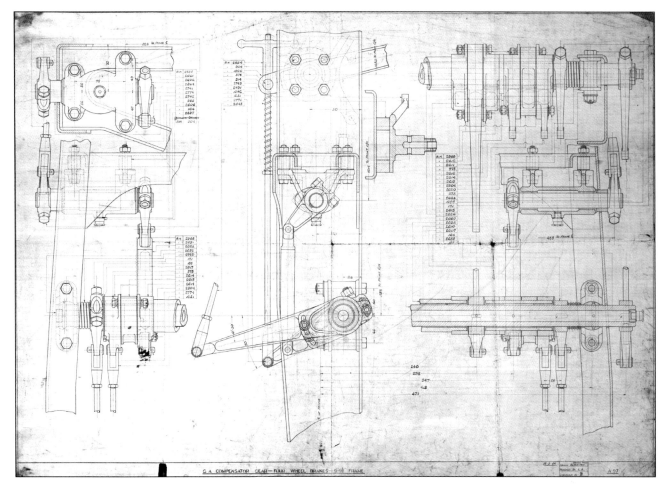

However, these exhibited high wear and could seize. The shafts were thus fixed in place, and the sliding motion transferred to the chassis frame bracket.

In the days before hydraulic brake systems a clever mechanical arrangement was fitted to limit the locking of one wheel due to chassis flexing or wear. The braking effort to each of the four individual wheels was equalised, using three compensators arranged on a transverse shaft and tube assembly mounted transversely across the chassis rails under the driver's seating position.

The first of the compensators split the brake pedal forces equally to each side of the car. This can be seen at the top right of the Bentley assembly drawing. The long lever to the left of this sub-section of the drawing was connected

via a rod to the brake pedal. A 'whiffle tree' (a shaft with three connected spherical profiles machined on it) conveyed the brake pedal force to the end flanges of the two tubes taking the pedal force to flanges on the cross-tubes near to the outer rails. The whiffle tree was free to rock and thus compensated for differing

ABOVE Brake compensator shaft assembly drawing. *(W.O. Bentley Memorial Foundation)*

RIGHT Brake compensator shaft. The casting behind the gearbox contains a recent after-market overdrive for motorway cruising. *(Andy Brown)*

torque in the left- and right-hand tubes, hence balancing the braking forces on each side of the car. At the left- and right-hand ends of the transverse tubes (the right-hand one being very short) were arranged two more whiffle tree arrangements which split the braking forces equally front to rear on either side of the car.

The two levers at the far right of the subassembly drawing were for the hand-lever actuation of the rear brakes. The outermost (far right) lever was connected by a rod to the hand-lever; the lever inboard of this was connected to a rod that connected to the right-rear shoes. The inner shaft shown in this subassembly carried the hand-lever input to a lever at the left-hand side of the cross-shaft assembly that then

in turn actuated the left rear shoes. But note that there was no attempt to balance the hand-lever brake forces side to side.

The handbrake lever, which was drilled for weight-saving purposes, was mounted outside the car to maximise space within the cockpit. Because two independent systems were a legal requirement at the time, the rear drums were fitted with two sets of shoes, one pair operated by the foot pedal and the other pair by the hand lever. Whilst the foot pedal activated the brakes on all four wheels, the hand lever only operated the independent pair of rear shoes. A ratchet on the hand lever could be engaged via a lever on the handbrake to keep the rear brakes locked for parking purposes.

The bottom of the handbrake lever connected via a rearward running rod to a lever connected to a shaft running through the centre of the brake compensator housing. Two further levers, just inboard of either chassis rail, were keyed to this shaft, then conveyed the handbrake lever input to the actuator barrels for the rear brakes.

'Halo' friction material was employed with the early, low-carbon ('mild') steel brake drums. In March 1928 the rate of brake wear was reduced by changing the material used for the brake drums from mild steel to carbon

steel with a 44% carbon content. This was then changed again to steel with 55% carbon content in the summer of 1930. Plans were also drawn up in the spring of 1928 to improve the braking so that when the brakes were applied and the front axle wound up on the front springs, the brakes would be pushed on even harder. (Previously the opposite had been the case, the effect of the front axle twisting on the springs being to reduce the front brake pressure.) This was achieved by simply reversing the front brake operating levers on the works racing cars.

The production version of this saw the original twin leading-edge shoes replaced by leading and trailing shoes (sometimes referred to as 'semi-servo' or 'self-wrapping') fitted to cars from 1929. This also involved fitting a stronger front axle to cope with the increased torque from the new brakes. The revised axle now had a reinforced H-shaped centre section and thicker material from the steering arm swivel housing inboard to the spring mounting point.

Wheels and tyres

The wheels (21in wire-spoked type) were manufactured by Rudge Whitworth of Coventry. The road cars were fitted with 5.25 x 21 tyres manufactured by Dunlop, while bigger tyres (6.75/7.00 x 21) were fitted to the race cars.

The wheels and tyres were balanced by fitting stacks of balance weights bolted through the centre of the rims, and/or by fitting lead weights around the outer ends of the spokes. The wheels were fitted to tapered splines at the ends of the axles, and held in place by a central double-eared lock nut.

Bodywork

Most of the racing Bentleys were classically known for their Vanden Plas open four-seater bodywork with cycle-type mudguards over the front wheels. The bonnet was formed from curved aluminium sheet, made in two halves and joined at a hinge that ran forward from the top of the bulkhead to the radiator along the car's centre line. A second hinge at the top of the vertical sides in each half of the bonnet allowed each side to fold flat when lifted. The bonnet was secured by a spring-loaded latch (with a finger loop to aid in lifting the catch) on either side, augmented by two leather straps. Louvres were cut in the bonnet to improve engine cooling (one way to tell a 4½-litre car from an earlier 3-litre version was that the side louvres formed one continuous row, whereas on the 3-litre they were arranged into separate front and rear groups). When the supercharged cars were found to overheat (at the 1930 Le Mans race), not only were the

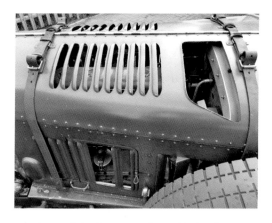

RIGHT Extra bodywork openings and louvre apertures for the supercharged engine, also showing bonnet-retaining spring-loaded catch and leather straps. *(Ian Wagstaff)*

BELOW General arrangement drawing supplied to coachbuilders by the Bentley Works for the purpose of matching the rear bodywork to the chassis. *(W.O. Bentley Memorial Foundation)*

apertures of the louvres enlarged but extra holes were also cut in the bonnet top and sides.

The body behind the bulkhead was supported by a wooden frame. The beams of this frame were screwed to each other rather than glued together, as glue joints would just crack due to the chassis flexing. Ash was used for the frame for the same reason, as less flexible wood would also crack. The wooden frame was then clad with thin aluminium panels, and the whole assembly clad with pre-coloured leather.

An alternative body was known as the

'Weymann Fabric Body'. This involved no metal cladding, the 'fabric' being applied directly to the wooden frame and then 'painted', in a similar fashion to how aircraft frames of the day were covered. This normally had a matt finish – contrasting with the gloss of the painted metal bonnet – but multiple coats of paint could be applied and then sanded and buffed to create a gloss finish, giving the impression (mistakenly) of metal bodywork. This finish was known as *tôle souplé*, the literal translation of which is 'sheet metal soft', which added to the misconception. Alternatively, and more commonly, the top layer of material would be made from colour-impregnated synthetic leather. This form of body was very light and flexible and hence eminently suitable for the race cars, but was not the most durable – less of a consideration when it comes to race car construction.

For the first appearance of the 4½-litre at Le Mans in 1927 (in prototype form) the 'traditional' body was run (with the full-length 'one piece' mudguards), as the rules required cars to run 'with the hood up' for the first three hours. The

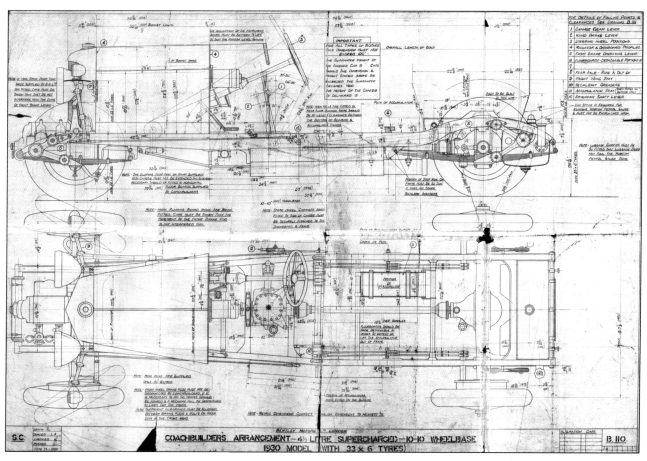

COACHBUILDERS ARRANGEMENT—4½ LITRE SUPERCHARGED—10-10 WHEELBASE 1930 MODEL (WITH 33 × 6 TYRES)

drivers were even required to erect the hood from its stowed position after sprinting across the track to their cars at the start of the race.

For 1928 the rear bodywork was modified into what is referred to as the 'bobtail' version of the car. The spare wheel was moved from being mounted relatively far forward on the right-hand side of the car and was now mounted vertically across the rear of the car. The top-rear body lines were then altered (and now manufactured from sheet aluminium) to match the outer diameter of the spare wheel at the rear of the car, making the cars look far more racy. This appearance was aided by individual motorcycle-type mudguards.

Only two (new) cars appeared in this format. The third car was the prototype returning from 1927, which retained its original open-tourer bodywork, including the long, one-piece mudguards. But it was this car that would go on to win, scoring the 4½-litre cars' only victory at the event. However, one of the 'bobtail' cars did set a new course record on the last lap of the race as Birkin attempted to make up for time lost changing a punctured tyre. His lap of 8min 7sec was 39sec less than the fastest lap set the year before.

These three cars returned to Le Mans for 1929, joined by a fourth 4½-litre car, fitted with open-tourer bodywork but with motorcycle-style mudguards and the spare wheel now just behind the left-hand front wheel. (It would also appear from photographs that one of the 'bobtail' cars reverted to bodywork like that of the prototype, with the spare wheel mounted

forward of the bulkhead on the right-hand side, but with motorcycle-style mudguards.)

With the requirement in 1927 that the first three hours of the Le Mans 24 Hours had to be driven with the hood fitted in the upright position, the car was fitted with a full-height, full-width windscreen (the front edge of the hood being latched on to the top edge of the windscreen frame). Windscreen wipers were not fitted, as the top 'half' of the windscreen was hinged along the top edge of the frame so that the bottom edge could be moved out and up until this top 'half' was horizontal. This provided the required visibility, otherwise the windscreen just became caked in mud from the road conditions of the time (which period windscreen-wipers could not have coped with anyway), and reduced aerodynamic drag.

From 1928 the rule requiring the hood to be deployed was abandoned, hence the windscreen was no longer required. ('Open-top' cars were still required to carry a hood, but it could be kept in the folded position.) The cars were thus fitted with a small 'aero-screen' in front of the driver, while a full-width wire mesh screen normally remained folded down in front of this. Should the hood need to be erected, the full-width mesh screen was 'stood up' and the front of the hood fixed to the top corners.

Interior

Dashboard

The racing car dashes were machined aluminium, while road car dashboards were

ABOVE LEFT Wire mesh windscreen. *(Andy Brown)*

ABOVE Rear bodywork wooden structure and thin alloy sheet and leather covering. *(Andy Brown)*

RIGHT Dashboard
instruments and
controls. *(Andy Brown)*

1 Speedometer
2 Clock
3 Fuel-line air pressure
gauge
4 Dashboard lighting
5 Fuel-tank air
pressure gauge
6 Oil pressure gauge
7 Fuel-tank pressure
pump
8 Horn
9 Light switches
10 Ammeter
11 Fuel-tank selector
12 Ignition spark timing
adjuster lever
13 Magnetos (on/off)
14 Water temprature
gauge
15 Oil temperature
gauge
16 Supercharger
pressure gauge
17 Ki-gass fuel primer
pump
18 Tachometer
19 Engine cooling fan
switch
20 Supercharger oil drip
feed indicators
21 Starter knob

RIGHT Dashboard
instruments and
controls. *(Andy Brown)*

generally made of wood. Included could
be such instruments as a clock, fuel-line air
pressure, oil pressure, fuel-tank pressure pump,
ammeter, fuel-tank selector, magnetos on/
off, speedometer, supercharger oil-drip feed
indicators, fan switch (a late addition due to the
cooling issues experienced by supercharged
cars), rev counter, Ki-gas fuel primer pump,
supercharger pressure and oil and water
temperature.

For racing purposes the clock had a small
window indicating time remaining, but this is
very difficult to see from the driving seat. A
counter from a billiard table was often installed
for the driver to be able to record the number
of laps covered during a race. A Wootton
lantern (a period torch) was carried as part of
the tool kit.

Pedals

In the 1920s, the position of the driver's
pedals had yet to be standardised by motor

RIGHT Clock, with
'Time to Go' window.
(Andy Brown)

FAR RIGHT Billiard
table 'lap counter'.
(Gill Wagstaff)

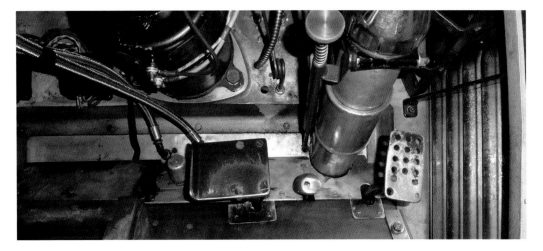

manufacturers. On the 4½-litre Bentley, for ease of 'packaging', the brake was the pedal furthest to the right, the accelerator (not much more than a small button) was in the middle, and the clutch pedal was on the left. The brake-pedal and clutch-pedal faces were drilled for lightening purposes.

The racing cars also featured an adjuster wheel (on the floor next to the gear lever) that could be used to take up the slack in the brake linkage that appeared as the brake shoes wore down.

Seats

The seats were fairly rudimentary by modern standards, but upholstered in good-quality leather. One novel feature adopted by the race team was to create a space where a tyre inner tube could be put inside the seat cushions; these could then be inflated to suit the comfort level required.

FAR LEFT Brake wear compensation wheel (arrowed).
(Andy Brown)

LEFT Tyre inner tube interior of seat cushion. *(Ian Wagstaff)*

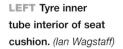

LEFT Wootton lantern used for night-time map reading or for peering under the bonnet at night if things haven't quite gone to plan.
(Ian Wagstaff)

Chapter Three

The driver's view

While the passage of time means that we can no longer speak to them, a number of the 'Bentley Boys' have left their thoughts on the 4½-litre in print. Thus we can still see the car through the eyes of a group of experienced individuals that ranged from a professional writer, Sammy Davis, to a professional driver, Frank Clement.

OPPOSITE 'From the first it was obvious that the 4½ was very fast indeed.' – S.C.H. Davis, Bentley factory driver. *(Ian Wagstaff)*

premises of Woolf Barnato, Sir Henry Birkin, Glen Kidston and Bernard Rubin.

Those who raced factory and/or independently entered 4½-litre cars in the long distance races of 1927 to 1930, after which the factory withdrew from competition, were: Woolf Barnato; Dr Dudley Benjafield; Jack Barclay; Sir Henry Birkin; Leslie Callingham; Jean Chassagne; Frank Clement; Humphrey Cook; S.C.H. Davis; Baron André d'Erlanger; George Duller; Jack Dunfee; M.O. Durand; George Eyston; Jack Field; Cecil Fiennes; Sir Roland Gunter; Eddie Hall; Beris Harcourt-Wood; E. Hayes; Nigel Holder; Earl (Francis) Howe; Glen Kidston; 'Bertie' Kensington Moir; Jack Patterson; Giulio Ramponi; Tim Rose-Richards; Bernard Rubin; Jill Scott; William Scott; and T.K. Williams. (See also Appendix 2.)

S.C.H. 'Sammy' Davis

S.C.H. 'Sammy' Davis was in the factory team for the 1927 Le Mans 24 Hours, sharing the winning 3-litre car with Dudley Benjafield. He observed, 'most important of all, the first of 4½-litres was to run in company with the two 3-litres. Thus, at last we had one big car, whereas in the past we had always been up against more powerful machinery'. By way of detail, he also pointed out that opening the oil filler on the new car automatically opened the level tap, saving one movement against the two of his own 3-litre.

ABOVE Only Clement and Callingham (left) raced a 4½-litre Bentley at Le Mans in 1927. However, the rest of that year's factory team, d'Erlanger, Duller, Davis and Benjafield, would drive such cars in subsequent seasons. *(W.O. Bentley Memorial Foundation)*

Even if they were not the first 'Bentley Boys' (strictly speaking those were the mechanics – see chapter four), the factory drivers were to become known as such, since many of them, at some stage, raced the company's 4½-litre model, whether in normally aspirated or supercharged form. In the main they can be regarded as playboy amateurs, although the experienced Frank Clement was a true professional driver. W.O. Bentley referred to them as 'sporting men of independent means' and they drove for no financial remuneration. Indeed, in London the south-east corner of Grosvenor Square even came to be known as 'Bentley Corner' thanks to the adjoining

RIGHT The Bentley Le Mans team for 1929. Left to right: d'Erlanger, Barnato, Birkin, Jack Dunfee, Kidston, Benjafield, Chassagne and Clement. *(Dr Ian Andrews collection)*

He was impressed by 'some wonderful lap times' that Frank Clement put in with the 4½-litre in practice. He also approved of the last-minute appointment of Leslie Callingham to replace Woolf Barnato, who had been held back in England on business, as the co-driver of the car. Callingham had already practised with 'the big car' and had 'worked most usefully with intense enthusiasm'. Their car, he said, appeared 'proudly bearing the number "one"'. 'From the first it was obvious that the 4½ was very fast indeed,' said Davis.

His first race in such a car was not to come until 1929 and the first Double Twelve race held at Brooklands, in which he shared the wheel with Sir Roland Gunter. 'My mount,' he wrote in his 1932 book *Motor Racing*, 'was to be one of the three 4½-litre Le Mans Bentleys.' He recalled that 'two of the 4½-litres were fitted with the light body which had evolved for Le Mans in 1928, a sort of shell with the spare wheel in the tail, slightly better streamlined that the ordinary touring bodies hitherto used'.

Davis recorded further details of the 1928 4½-litre cars: 'All … had enormous fuel tank fillers with the cam and lever securing device, and no screw threads whatever. The wire gauze windscreens were made to conform to the shape of the scuttle, on which they lay horizontally except when the hood was up, driver and mechanic being protected by two small glass screens of aeroplane type.'

He continued: 'Another interesting gadget had been evolved; the opening of the lid to the oil filler still opened the crank case level tap, but shutting that lid did not close the tap, through which oil continued to flow until the driver pressed down the clutch pedal to engage first speed, interconnecting levers then shutting the tap. The idea was excellent as, with the previous device, even if the driver stopped pouring the moment oil showed at the drain hole, too much oil was likely to reach the sump, a thing entirely obviated by the delay action of the new design. A sort of frying pan was also provided which the driver, or mechanic, slid under the sump to catch the overflowing oil, this preventing the track in front of the pit from becoming impossibly slippery in the course of time.

'A new type of can was also produced which contained the oil for refilling the spare oil tank, a

valve automatically opening when the can was placed in the spare oil tank filler, thus avoiding the delay when the mechanic had to pour in the oil in person.'

It was not all high technology. 'The principal problem peculiar to this race was caused by the cars having to be left for a night in the open in between the two sections of the race, and yet kept sufficiently warm for the engines to be started with starting motors on the drop of the flag in the morning.' (Typical of Brooklands, the Double Twelve – which took place in two 12-hour segments in order not to infuriate the locals – was to be decided on handicap. That, said Davis, made the result difficult to call, but 'the three 4½s were likely to finish at a really good speed.') 'Our arrangements were to provide old army blankets with which to wrap up bonnet and radiator completely, and apparatus for heating the lubricating oil before the sump was refilled.'

L.V. Head, his mechanic, and Davis allotted a spare 4½-litre engine for practice, 'slaving away at changing rockers, changing valve springs or replacing and retiming a magneto, until we had the thing off by heart as an exact routine'. Leading Bentley mechanic Wally Hassan had suggested that the engine be thoroughly warmed up beforehand, but that was unanimously rejected 'as we wanted some skin on our hands during the race!' Practising wheel changing led to Davis having a specially heavy Rudge-wheel copper hammer made, 'the effect of which was excellent'.

ABOVE 'Sammy' Davis (see here in his familiar Basque beret) had a varied career, including acting as team manager for MG at Le Mans in 1955. *(Marcus Chambers)*

Davis recalled that he did not want to push the 4½-litre too hard at first. The engine temperature was lower than he would have liked and the hood, which had to be erect for the opening ten laps, was standing up 'against a force "20" gale if we went up to 102 mph!' For tactical reasons, Davis continued beyond the ten laps before coming in to lower the hood. 'When we did, neither Head nor I could for a moment release the hood from the windscreen, did not in fact succeed until we had carefully prised one catch out, but the delay seemed immense.'

Sticking strictly to a rev limit that had been given him, Davis did his best to give the 4½-litre 'as easy a run as possible'. On the second day he started out using just 2,000rpm but increased this to 3,500rpm after a couple of hours to remain competitive. Despite a concern over oil pressure and, at one point, an undone catch that caused the bonnet to lift slightly, 'the old 4½ travelled well'.

The last half hour of the race Davis described as 'wildly exciting'. One of his car's rear tyres was disintegrating, but there was no time for a pit stop if he were to win. It was all so close at the end, with the 4½-litre beaten by just .003 on the formula calculation by one of the Alfa Romeos, after a total of 24 hours. After the race, the loss of oil on the second day was found to be due to a defective washer on the pressure filter's lid. David would race once more in a 4½-litre car, sharing with Clive Dunfee in the 1929 Brooklands 500. Although there would be further drives in a factory-entered Bentley, they would be in a Speed Six.

Sir Henry 'Tim' Birkin

Some of the thoughts of Sir Henry Birkin with regard to the Bentley 4½-litre can be gleaned from his famous, and initially controversial, autobiography *Full Throttle*. However, it has to be remembered that the book was ghost-written in just three short weeks by a teenager who would later admit that he was ignorant about cars (see pages 78–79).

Birkin stated that he 'felt … indeed lucky to be at the wheel of 4½-litre unsupercharged number three' for Le Mans in 1928. He also wrote how he drove the supercharged version of the 4½-litre Bentley for the first time at Le Mans in 1929 'and had no success'. W.O. may have disapproved of the blown cars but these were Birkin's project, so it is perhaps no surprise that it states in *Full Throttle* 'that to transmit the higher power of a supercharger involves much redesigning of engines, but the difference in speed between the "blown" and "unblown" Bentley is a difference between 125 and 108mph, and more than worth the trouble.' He almost expresses relief that the supercharger 'was approved [in time for the second round of the Anglo-Italian Tournament at Brooklands]; it had only just been fitted, and meant an increase of 100hp – 35 of which it required for itself – and a far swifter acceleration.' He admitted, though, that when Rudi Caracciola was entered for the Tourist Trophy in his 7-litre Mercedes-Benz, 'my 4½-litre Bentley, though supercharged too, stood little chance when we both started from scratch'.

It was mainly Birkin who competed at Brooklands with the muscular 4½-litre single-seater Bentley, converted from one of the Paget 'Blower' cars, saddened that there were no longer any British-built cars with which he could contest the major Continental events. Towards the end of *Full Throttle* he recalls: 'There was a long-standing argument about my single-seater Bentley with its great speed and John Cobb's

RIGHT Birkin with his trademark polka-dot scarf. *(W.O. Bentley Memorial Foundation)*

Delage with its wonderful acceleration. My car had a 4½-litre capacity, and his a 10½-litre; but though we had often been involved in exciting races together, we had never had the course to ourselves. This was now to be granted; and a match, like the old horse-racing matches, was arranged between the two rivals, the English and the French, for a purse of a hundred sovereigns.'

The Delage's greater acceleration enabled it to lead the first of the three laps around Brooklands. 'I tried not to lift my foot once from the accelerator on the next round, and as we went over the famous bump, the Bentley gave a terrific heave.' On the final lap, as the pair 'came off the Members' Banking I felt the Bentley, as it were, hang above [the Delage] for an instant and then shoot ahead … It was a thrilling race, and the long, red single-seater never went better.'

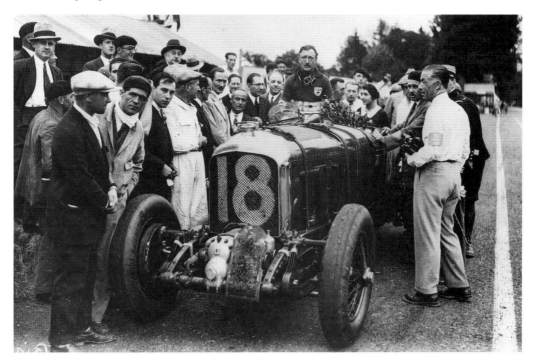

THE WRITING OF *FULL THROTTLE*

Sir Henry Birkin's autobiography, *Full Throttle* was to inspire future racing drivers. Innes Ireland mentioned in his own autobiography, *All Arms and Elbows*, that he was given a copy by an elderly lady who owned a 3-litre Bentley. 'It inspired my dreams and I imagined myself doing the things Birkin had done.'

However, the book was actually ghost-written by a dropout from Oxford University, Michael Burn, who had found himself in the summer of 1932 in the French resort of Le Touquet, favourite resort of 'rich and fashionable people'. There he was captivated by the guests at a party hosted by Syrie Maugham, ex-wife of author Somerset Maugham. One of these was Birkin, 'in love', says 'Micky', with another guest, socialite Sylvia Ashley, whose five husbands included Georgian noble Prince Djordjadze, a winner of the 1931 Spa 24 Hours in a Mercedes-Benz SSK. Burn was meant to return to New College for a second year, but had not done any work and was 'beginning to get scared'. He recalled: 'I was 19 and wanted to be a writer.'

Birkin told him that he had been asked to compile his autobiography and, even though he had only just met Burn, he asked him if he would like to write it. Then Birkin rang his publisher, G.T. Foulis, to be told that it was too late. If the book was to be ready for Christmas it had to be written in the next three weeks. Burn would later confess that he knew nothing about cars, notwithstanding that his second tome was a history of Brooklands, *Wheels Take Wings*. He went on to write about 20 books (as well as becoming *The Times*' youngest foreign editor),

> 3 & 5, Burlington Gardens,
> London, W.1.
>
> 4th November, 1932.
>
> Michael Clive Burn Esq.,
>   8, Hyde Park Square,W.2.
>
> Dear Sir,
>
>   I hereby confirm the arrangement made between us in consideration of the work which you have done in writing "Full Throttle," namely that I will pay to you or cause to be paid to you out of any Royalties to which I may become entitled under an Agreement dated the 20th October 1932 and made between G.T. Foulis & Co.Ltd., Publishers of 7, Milford Lane, Strand,London and myself, 25% upon the first 5,000 copies, 33 1/3rd % upon the next 15,000 copies and 40% upon any additional copies sold, and I hereby authorise you to notify Messrs.G.T. Foulis & Co.Ltd., of this arrangement.
>
>   It is understood that this Agreement applies to sales of the book or its rights in the British Empire or abroad and also to the cheaper editions as and when published. And furthermore that I shall be under no obligation to pay to you any of the Royalties until received by me from Messrs. G.T. Foulis & Co.Ltd.,
>
>   Yours faithfully,
>
>   *Henry. R.S.Birkin.*

LEFT Birkin wrote to Burn in the November of 1932 to confirm their agreement with regard to *Full Throttle*. Many decades later Haynes Publishing was to acquire the G.T. Foulis name.

and none of the others have had anything to do with cars.

Perhaps ignorance really is bliss, for Burn and Birkin took up the challenge when others might have baulked at the thought. Most of the work was carried out at Burn's parents' London home, with Birkin 'striding up and down and dictating' and Burn furiously taking notes. Looking back, Micky was amused that anyone should think that the literary style, certainly of the first part of *Full Throttle*, could have been written by Birkin.

Burn's father, Sir Clive, writing about his son in a letter soon after publication, said: 'I think it is an amusing effort for a boy of 19 and holds your attention upon a damned dull subject.'

Burn recalled that Birkin took him to Brooklands and drove him round the track. He thinks that it may have been in the single-seater, but 'that can't have been, can it?' he said.

Burn was destined to have a career every bit as adventurous as that of Birkin. He confessed to some unsavoury acquaintances before the war, including spy Guy Burgess, and was introduced to Hitler by Unity Mitford, initially being duped by the way in which the Nazis had reduced Germany's unemployment problem. He was not misled for long, indeed his politics swung in the opposite direction, and with the coming of war he found himself an officer on the daring commando raid on St Nazaire, where he was captured.

By 1943 Burn was incarcerated in Colditz. If he found himself in Colditz, surely he must have been a would-be escaper? 'No,' he said; he did his bit listening to the wireless and looking out for guards. He was never sure whether it was because the Germans knew he had met Hitler, or because a spy in one of his previous camps had told them he was giving lectures on communism to fellow prisoners, that he ended up in the infamous castle.

Burn returned to *The Times* after the war, working in Vienna and Budapest before leaving the paper in the early 1950s to become a full-time writer. In 2006 he wrote to one of the authors, 'I still know nothing about cars, but at 93 still drive – a Proton. "Tim" would have been disgusted.'

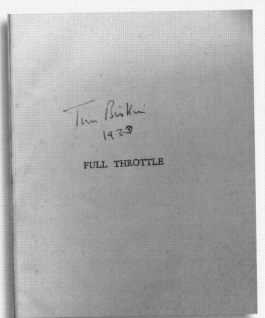

FULL THROTTLE

By

Sir Henry ("Tim") Birkin, Bt

Foreword by

The Rt. Hon. The Earl Howe,
P.C., C.B.E., V.D.

G T FOULIS & CO LTD
Henley-on-Thames
Oxfordshire

Dr J. Dudley Benjafield

Harley Street surgeon Benjafield's first race in a Bentley 4½-litre came in the 1928 Essex Six Hours, when he and Bernard Rubin finished second. However, he pointed out how he had had a hand in who drove the sole such car at Le Mans the previous year. The decision to run one alongside two 3-litres came late in the day and meant a rearrangement of the drivers. The 4½ was seen as the 'first string' member of the team and that meant that Frank Clement, as Bentley's number one driver, should be transferred to its seat. Then, to Benjafield's dismay, Davis was suggested as his co-driver. 'I refused point blank to this,' recalled Benjafield after the war. 'Undoubtedly, it was very selfish of me, but since the basis of the whole affair had been No 7 (a 3-litre) and I had been fixed with Sammy at least nine months previously to share the driving with me, I felt quite justified. I was very grateful to Sammy for backing me up in this crisis, since there could be no possible doubt that the new car must have a far better chance of winning than a car which was smaller and slower.'

Eventually, 'after a great deal of argument', it was settled that Leslie Callingham should be at the wheel of the 4½. (Davis' loyalty was,

of course, rewarded, with the battered No 7 staggering to the line to win while the 4½ sat in a ditch.) That year's race had, as Benjafield pointed out, 'a comparatively poor' entry, with 'the 4½-litre the biggest car in the race'.

The following year Benjafield himself was teamed with Clement as part of the all-4½-litre entry, driving a car numbered 2. Said Benjafield, 'Nos 2 and 3 were both new cars specially built for the race … There was nothing to choose in the matter of speed between Nos 2 and 3, and they had only a very slight advantage over no 4 [the survivor of the 1927 White House crash] in this respect.'

It was, though, Barnato and Rubin, 'the third string in the team and definitely the slowest', who won, having 'enjoyed a trouble-free run, never having opened the bonnet'. Continued Benjafield: 'The chief reasons for this immunity to minor troubles was the fact that they were content to travel at a speed a little below their maximum and let others bask in the limelight during the early stages of the race.'

Benjafield was back in a 4½-litre the following year at La Sarthe, which he followed in 1930 by being a member of Birkin's supercharged team, making him one of the most experienced Bentley 4½-litre drivers at Le Mans. He wrote that his car for 1929 'was the 4½-litre which had won the Double Twelve a Brooklands', before correcting himself by pointing out that while the car was 'first on speed' the event was run as a handicap and that, driven by Davis and Roland Gunter, it had been classified in second place.

For 1930 the factory cars were all 6½-litres, but Benjafield was now part of Birkin's supercharged 4½-litre team, later pointing out his involvement in the origins of this car. 'During the autumn and early winter of 1929, Tim Birkin, assisted by many others, notably H. Kensington Moir, Bernard Rubin, Beris Harcourt-Wood, Clive Gallop, and Captain W.O. Bentley on the technical side, put into practice a scheme which had been incubating in the minds of most of us for some considerable time, viz, to supercharge the 4½. The germ of the idea had been sown in my mind as long ago as November 1924, by Captain W.O. Bentley himself.'

Following the 1930 Le Mans there was talk that the 'blown' 4½-litres may have been

BELOW Benjafield and not Birkin drove the Paget single-seater in the 1931 BRDC 500-miles. Bevan and Couper's 4½-litre Bentley is above them on the Brooklands banking. (W.O. Bentley Memorial Foundation)

sacrificial entries, 'hares' to entice the German drivers into over-stressing their Mercedes-Benz. Benjafield was to emphatically deny this. 'All the sensational rubbish published in the press about elaborate team tactics adopted by the two Bentley groups to "crack up" the Mercedes, are entirely without foundation in fact. Is it likely that any "team tactics", however subtle and however brilliant, would direct one of its team to continue racing with a car weighing over 2¼ tons at speeds of up to 130mph on bare canvas, having thrown the tread two or three miles before the place where the car could have been stopped? Nothing but the individual sheer dare-devilry or our beloved Tim would do this sort of thing. Madness, yes, but rather admirable madness. Tim's driving was brilliant, but very hard on the car – furthermore he could never resist the temptation to play to the gallery in the early stages of a race.' So, there you have it – or do you? Over a decade earlier, Birkin had written, 'It was obvious to both of us ['Tim' himself and Bentley] that a car must be detailed to wear down the Mercedes, make it use its supercharger – which is engaged by a clutch – and so overstrain its engine and put it out of the race … The three official Bentleys were told to give me every opening for a clear run.'

There was, though, one thing on which Benjafield and Birkin agreed: the latter's attitude. 'The policy of wearing down was one after my own heart,' wrote Sir Henry, 'and I promised to exploit it with all my ability, on the one condition exacted as a *quid pro quo* for Dorothy Paget. I made W.O. agree not to race the second supercharged Bentley with the official team, if at the end of the race either of the others had a chance of victory.'

Frank Clement

The only professional driver amongst the Bentley Boys, Frank Clement was also one of the most successful when it came to long-distance races with a 4½-litre. Only he and Barnato scored more than one endurance win with what he described as a 'marvellous car'.

In her book *The Other Bentley Boys*, Elizabeth Nagle quoted Clement's memory of the 4½-litre's initial testing. 'I don't think we had

any trouble with that first 4½,' he recalled. 'We put it in a long 3-litre chassis and, with a friend, I went over to Le Mans to get the gear ratios we wanted. We went round and round that circuit I don't know how many times before I was satisfied. It was a very nice car. It went like a scalded cat and, after the 3-litre, it was a real joy to drive.'

LEFT Frank Clement, Bentley's only professional driver, was described by W.O. as 'an impressible optimist'. *(W.O. Bentley Memorial Foundation)*

BELOW Frank Clement and Jean Chassagne were teamed up in a 4½-litre for the 1929 Le Mans. *(W.O. Bentley Memorial Foundation)*

Clement shared the sole 4½-litre when the car made its racing debut at Le Mans in 1927, arranging with his 3-litre teammates that they should look out for him after about 13 laps. 'Well,' said Clement, 'that 4½ was a very fast car.' He caught the other Bentleys within 12 laps, some time before they were expecting him, and he had difficulty getting past. 'I just couldn't get them out of the way.'

His horn was not much help. 'We tried every type you could think of for Le Mans, even one driven from the flywheel, and none was any good. Anyway, I eventually got by, and when I came to hand over W.O. asked me if I'd struck any trouble. It was rather amusing when I had to say, "only from my own people".'

Clement enjoyed those early laps. 'I was the fastest car in the race by far, doing a maximum of over a hundred, against about 90mph on the 3-litres.' He even managed to break the lap record with the hood up (a requirement for the opening laps). That, he said, 'showed what a powerful car it was'.

It all came to naught following the infamous White House crash, but two months later Clement, partnered by George Duller, took the first 4½-litre to Montlhéry. There, as Clement recalled, 'we won easily in spite of the twisty course which was very unsuitable for the 4½.'

The following year Clement was back at Le Mans with a new 4½-litre. 'That was … when we discovered we had trouble with the 4½ frames … my front door kept opening, and I had to keep leaning across and slamming it shut.' That was not all. 'Suddenly, I was overheating badly. I stopped and found that the radiator hose had gone, and, with it, most of the water.' As water could only be taken every 20 laps, that meant retirement. 'Afterwards, we found the frame had cracked, and was so badly distorted that everything was out of line – hence the trouble with the door.'

Clement would, however, win one more time with a 4½-litre Bentley when he and Jack Barclay took the 1929 Brooklands 500-miles.

Post-war observations

Such has been the enthusiasm of Bentley owners that many 4½-litre cars have been raced since the Second World War in club events. Their numbers are, understandably, dwindling, and as their value increases so does the care with which they are driven. Perhaps only Martin Overington (see pages 118–119) still races one in the true sense of the word.

'At Le Mans,' he observes, 'the car will naturally understeer.' To get it to oversteer and to compensate for the fact that the brakes are so bad, Overington double-declutches into third

BELOW Martin Overington's exhaust glows brightly as night falls on the Le Mans Classic. (*Colin Murrell*)

at really high rpm, keeping his foot pressed on the clutch so that the engine revs drop until he enters the corner. He then drops the clutch; the flywheel is so heavy that he gets braking out of this, and the back of the car snatches out. 'The back has now gone light, which means the car can now be oversteered.'

Continues Overington: 'On a long left-hander, such as the Porsche Curves at Le Mans, it runs out of oil. You feather the throttle off slightly and wait for the corner to straighten out. The half seals always go. By the end of a Le Mans Classic you have useless brakes; they are covered in oil. The brakes are pretty useless anyway.

'I can do the downshifts on the Bentley exceedingly quickly. It's like a knife through butter. But the upshifts, especially third to fourth, are really slow. The only way to do this is to grit your teeth and bang it through. I've only had one gearbox build and there was barely a burr on the back of the gears.'

For a while, Overington also owned a Bugatti T35, which 'essentially you drove in silk gloves with your fingertips. The Bentley you drive with your fists in boxing gloves. It's a real British bulldog of a car in every way.'

At the 2012 Le Mans Classic meeting, Overington shared his Blower with an illustrious name. Of those who raced a 4½-litre Bentley in period, eight (Barnato, Benjafield, Birkin,

Clement, Davis, Howe, Rubin and Kidston) were to win the Le Mans 24 Hours, although only Barnato and Rubin were to come first driving such a car. To their number can now be added another, five-times Le Mans winner Derek Bell.

'I have the greatest respect for all the guys that raced them in the period,' says Bell. 'Those guys that drove them for 24 hours at Le Mans were amazing – from a physical point more than anything else, because the cars are not particularly fast. Shifting gear is not easy and it must have been very wearing. [The gearbox on Martin Overington's car is easier to use than the one on the factory's team car.] Since then I have learnt that some people have straight-through gears that fall into place like a Hewland. The Blower is the car that I have particularly got to

ABOVE His Kop Hill run over, Doug Hill returns to the paddock via the roads of Princes Risborough. *(Ian Wagstaff)*

LEFT Martin Overington's 'Blower' appeared at the first Bicester Flywheel event in 2015. *(Ian Wagstaff)*

<!-- caption -->**ABOVE** In addition to racing Martin Overington's car at the 2012 Le Mans Classic, Derek Bell has also driven Bentley Motors' own 'Blower' on the Ennstal Classic.
(Ennstal Classic)

know and love but it has taken me four years to really enjoy it.

'You really have to think coming up to corners. You have got to start thinking about your braking at a certain point, as it only stops at a certain rate and you will not lock the brakes up – you will just go off the road. With the central throttle pedal, you can't heel and toe. You have to hit the foot on to the brake, come off and whack it on to the gas pedal and then back on to the brake again, which is very upsetting for the car. In the meantime, you haven't slowed down much as you have been trying to get into gear. It's really difficult to get into a rhythm.

'The Bugattis and Alfas of the time were much easier to drive. The dear old Bentley is certainly very agricultural, but very strong, and with an amazing character. I look down this long green bonnet and see the straps over it and think, "This

is fantastic." They built these cars, raced them at Le Mans and then, in some cases, drove them home. They are just amazing cars.'

Derek observes that the Le Mans Classic is a 'wonderful event, particularly for people who have never done it as a main race'. After 26 races there he has, though, no need to go back. The opportunities to see a Le Mans 24 Hours winner racing a Bentley 4½-litre at La Sarthe will remain rare. Having said that, Bell does observe that 'I initially wasn't happy in one, but now I have learnt so much about the Bentleys that I would love to drive them again.'

An example of the more immediate post-war generation when the cars tended to be raced with more verve is Bentley Drivers Club stalwart Harvey Hine, who drove pre-war racer Harry Rose's 4½-litres, both supercharged and normally aspirated. 'Harry was like a second father to me,' he recalls.

'Everybody used to say that the Blowers did not handle but I used to set it up myself on the tyre pressures up to 55psi in the front and 45psi in the back. I then set the shock absorbers up and I had perfectly good handling after that; I could drive it round on the throttle.

'In order to satisfy Mrs Rose, who was watching at Woodcote, I used to have to put the back out on to the grass [this was the old Club circuit, sharp right-hand Woodcote]. If she did not see the dust she would think I was not trying.' Hine remembers that the 4½-litre, though, was not competitive on a tight track such as the old Silverstone Club.

RIGHT Harvey Hine in the family 4½-litre. 'I remember being driven to school in it.'
(Harvey Hine collection)

'It was important to get the engine hot before you started. The key thing was to try and get it warmed enough so that you could only just put your hand on the engine bearer. The car generated a huge amount of heat; you certainly could not drive it in plimsolls, because the clutch pedal would melt the rubber sole. You had to use leather soles.

'It was a lovely car to handle. It was taut, but the gearbox was dreadfully noisy. I could only have a conversation with a passenger when I was in top gear. Driving on the road was dreadful if it was wet as it only had a vacuum windscreen wiper – and with a supercharged car there was no vacuum! However, if you get a car like this to handle well on the road it will also drive well on the track.'

Despite its Le Mans-style body, the National Motor Museum's Bentley 4½-litre has never been raced. Nevertheless, the museum's manager Doug Hill has driven the car many thousands of miles across the continent of Europe. He observes: 'It's a heavy car to drive and W.O.'s way of compensating for the weight of the supercharger at the front was to fit a bigger steering wheel. The gear change is an absolute delight. I have now been driving the car for 40 years and it is difficult to teach anyone to change gear as you do it intuitively. The standard double-declutch principle applies but you vary that with the temperature of the gearbox and the road conditions. You really have to "read" the car. It's a car you strap on.

'My favourite stretch of road with the car is the Col Turini; you can get into a beautiful rhythm going up. Selvio is also a great road for it. Going up is quite easy, because you can slide the back out, but going down is difficult because it understeers. You have to be careful if you slide the back of a Bentley, because of the way that the loading works on the rear axle.'

Harvey contends that the 'Blowers' should not understeer. This, he says, is only likely to happen due to poor set-up, most likely the caster angle, as this is what governs the attitude of the rear end.

RIGHT No stranger to such cars, Prince Michael of Kent is seen here shortly after driving Karen Mann's 4½-litre at the 2016 Windsor Castle Concours of Elegance. (Ian Wagstaff)

ABOVE Doug Hill about to tackle Kop Hill near Princes Risborough in the National Motor Museum's 4½-litre. (Colin West)

BELOW Overington's 'Blower' proudly indicates not only Martin's ownership of the famed Hôtel de France at La Chartre near Le Mans but also the fact that it has been raced by Derek Bell. (Gill Wagstaff)

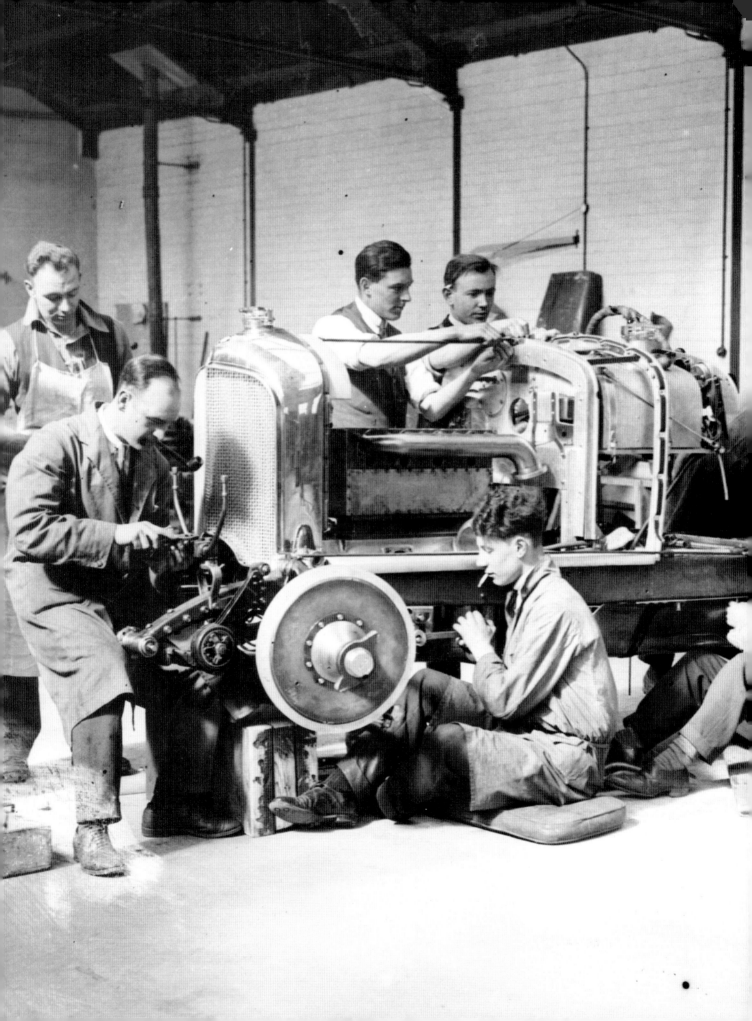

Chapter Four

The mechanic's view

The factory mechanics were called 'the Bentley Boys' before the sobriquet was applied to the drivers. Where, with the exception of Frank Clement, the latter were all amateurs, the mechanics were true professionals, ensuring that the marque remained true to its reputation for reliability. Thanks mainly to author Elizabeth Nagle, a number have left their memories of their time with Bentley.

OPPOSITE 'Birkin didn't expect his "Blower" to last the full race.' – Leslie Pennal, Bentley mechanic.
(W.O. Bentley Memorial Foundation)

The Bentley team mechanics

As far as other Haynes racing car Owners' Workshop Manuals have been concerned, it has been possible to interview many of that crucial but largely unsung breed of men who acted as mechanics on the cars. But the passage of time means that this has not been possible in this case. However, Elizabeth Nagle has left us an invaluable record of the original 'Bentley Boys' in her book *The Other Bentley Boys*, which was published in 1964 when many of them were still alive.

One of the now best remembered, Walter Hassan, joined Bentley in 1921 straight from technical school, becoming an integral part of the company's racing activities. He was to become one of motor sport's most eminent engineers, eventually heading up Coventry Climax's rise to Formula One World Championship success.

As far as Hassan was concerned, 1927 was looked on as the 'first real year' for the team. Before, they had only 'played at it'. This, of course, was the first year for the 4½-litre and, Hassan recalled, this meant one less problem. Being only 4cc short of the maximum for the 3-litre class, the earlier cars had to be examined by an RAC scrutineer in the UK on behalf of the ACU before they could compete at Le Mans. At 4,398cc, the capacity of the 4½-litre was

HOTEL MODERNE
LE MANS 1926

TO COLIN FROM
Bill Rockell

FREDDIE FOX
STORES

HAROLD EASTON
RACING MECH.

NOBBY CLARKE
FOREMAN

BOBBY BIGGS
SHOP BOY

ARTHUR SAUNDERS
CHIEF RACING
MECH.

MR HEAD (CAPUT)
JOURNALIST

WALLY SAUNDERS
RACING MECH.

BILL ROCKELL
ENGINE SHOP

LESLIE PENNAL
RACING MECH.

nowhere near as critical and there was no need for such examination.

'The 4½-litre Le Mans engine was easy to remember,' recalled Hassan. 'Using the 31.535 road-racing tyre, and a 3.3 to 1 back-axle ratio, their speed was exactly 100mph at 3,500rpm; bhp 118.'

Hassan was on duty for the 4½-litre's first win, the Montlhéry 24 Hours, and involved in what driver Frank Clement reckoned was 'a rather hair-raising experience'. On the morning of the second day, one of the seams of the car's 40-gallon petrol tank had split; fuel had dripped on to the hot exhaust pipe and appeared to set fire to the tank. There was not much that could be done about the leak and Hassan suggested shortening the exhaust pipe and taking the floorboards out of the back so that Clement could see if it would fire again. That did not work; a vacuum formed in the back of the car, sucking the fumes in and threatening Clement with carbon-monoxide poisoning. On top of that the car caught fire again, although the driver managed to put it out with his Pyrene fire extinguisher.

Hassan then came up with a better idea that involved 'a scoop thing' wired over the exhaust pipe, which re-routed the fumes on to the ground and away from the cockpit.

'It was quite a fire,' remembered Hassan, 'and when Frank Clement and I were both hard at it, squirting like mad, the first time, something very funny happened. There was a terrific explosion, and, of course, we both shot miles up the track before we turned round to see what was left: you accelerate no end when petrol's about.' The pair was covered in white dust but the fire was out. 1926 RAC Grand Prix winner Robert Sénèschal, who was marshalling for the race, was laughing 'like hell'. He had fired 'one of those explosive-type extinguishers' at the car but failed to warn them.

Hassan has also left his views on the frame trouble that the 4½-litres experienced at the 1928 Le Mans (see Clement's comments on page 82). He pointed out that it was not confined to the two cars that suffered during the race itself. 'All three went in the end, because the car that got through the race without frame trouble ... only just did. If I remember rightly,' he said, 'the frame went when I was driving it back

from the coast to London. Then exactly the same thing happened as it had to the others – and I lost all the water. I think it was something to do with the frames twisting – I don't recollect exactly what the trouble was.'

Wally Saunders, whose father Arthur had been a racing mechanic in the early days at Brooklands and who worked on the Bentley factory team right through its racing years, had a suggestion 'that those cars didn't have any strut gears then. I can certainly remember something about it, and that was the reason the frames went.' A study of photographs indicates that Saunders was correct. Indeed, Bentley himself concurred and pointed out that the race had 'exposed the weakness [which]

(see Clement's comments on page 82)

ABOVE The real Bentley Boys at Le Mans in 1929. Standing, left to right: unknown Birkin mechanic, 'Papa' David from the Hôtel Moderne, Chevrollier, Wally Hassan, Jack Selway, Major Williams, Nobby Clarke, Collier and Puddephat. Seated, left to right: Pryke and Howard. *(W.O. Bentley Memorial Foundation)*

BELOW YW 5758 outside the racing shop at Kingsbury prior to the 1929 Le Mans, in which it eventually finished a troubled fourth having been the leading 4½-litre at half-distance. *(Dr Ian Andrews collection)*

was, of course, immediately rectified thereafter'. (Saunders was to act as a mechanic for Bill Mason's Bentley 4½-litre during the 1950s.)

It is interesting to note that even in the earliest days of motor sport, manufacturers protected their reputations and limited the media's knowledge of their failures. It is known that the works employed code so that telegrams could be sent calling for spares as required by the owners. That way if telegrams were intercepted they were meaningless. At Le Mans, in 1928, two chassis did indeed fail, one during the race and the other on the way home. However, the second car to fail in the race, chassis number KM 3088, we now know did not suffer from a broken chassis frame. The car was destined for Le Mans the following year and so had a replacement heavy chassis fitted post-race to negate the known failure.

The original frame was recycled into a standard 4½, which was common practice at that time in the company's history. This original 1928 Le Mans frame was recently discovered by William Medcalf and, following detailed examination and non-destructive crack testing, the myth of a broken chassis has been put to bed. Curiously a photograph taken prior to the race, in the Team's hotel car park at Le Mans, shows KM 3088 with its valve chest removed, which is quite major surgery. In view of the confirmation of the integrity of its chassis it would be more plausible to think that this car suffered from valve gear failure. Rather than having two separate component failures that year, it may have been advantageous to place the blame on the circuit, which was poorly prepared, with a diagonal ridge across a fast section that damaged many cars. Although the team would have been aware of the reason for the car's failure, damage limitation would have been paramount at the time. Probably, out of loyalty to W.O. and his fellow teammates, Hassan maintained his position even decades later.

'Nobby' Clarke was the first mechanic on the Bentley payroll and it was he who recalled that the idea to build up a spare car for Le Mans from racing parts properly started with the prototype 4½-litre, YW 3774. 'We always took a spare or practice car with us, and it occurred to us that it would be far more sensible to drive heavy parts, like axles, to Le Mans as a car, rather than carry

them.' The idea had, actually, first been used back in 1922 for the Tourist Trophy and in the 1927 Le Mans with chassis 976.

A riding mechanic was called for in some of the races, a tradition that went back to the earliest days of motor racing but which would soon become a thing of the past. Hassan recalled that he was asked to accompany Bernard Rubin in one of the Paget 'Blower' 4½-litres in the 1929 TT. 'I wouldn't ride with him, he was a shocker.' The management was not happy about this but Hassan pointed out that he had built the Speed Six that was being driven by Glen Kidston and that was the car he was interested in. Kidston backed him up and Birkin's usual mechanic accompanied Rubin. In the event Rubin rolled his 'Blower', but thankfully the mechanic was short and came to no harm as the car turned over. 'By golly,' Hassan later exclaimed, 'if I'd been in it, I'd have had my head knocked off.'

Hassan was to have his own 'moment' with a 4½-litre in 1928. He was driving the winning car to Paris from Le Mans when a rear wheel fell off. A problem with the spokes meant that the Rudge-Whitworth locking ring unscrewed and the wheel parted company from the car. Hassan reflected on the fact that some 30 to 40 miles earlier it had still been competing in the race. 'I think that there was quite a row with the wheel people over that, and that the next wheels to be fitted had solid hubs so that half the front spokes took some of the torque.'

The mechanics had their own views on the tactic allegedly used in the 1930 Le Mans. As far as Hassan was concerned, it was Barnato that broke the Mercedes challenge. 'I've always thought it nonsense to say that Birkin [in a 'Blower' 4½-litre] did as well, because, in fact, he burst himself and fell out. It was Barnato and the race strategy that beat the Mercedes, and the skill with which he drove the Speed Six to orders. Of course, in that race Birkin was driving for himself in his private "Blower" team, so he could run the race the way he wanted.'

Another of the senior mechanics, Leslie Pennal, was not present at the race, but from conversations he later heard believed differently. Sammy Davis, he recalled, had said that it was 'jolly sporting of Birkin possibly to sacrifice his car like that'. Davis had told Pennal about a

meeting of both the factory and Paget team drivers before the race, which had discussed tactics, something that was confirmed by Dudley Benjafield. It was known that the German drivers did not want to use their supercharger too often if their car was to last, and so Birkin volunteered to make them do just that. Pennal admitted though that 'Birkin didn't expect his "Blower" to last the full race in any case – that was pretty common knowledge too.'

The spirit of the original 'Bentley Boys' lives on in specialist operations such as the Kingsbury Racing Shop, Vintage Bentley Heritage and NDR. Colin Smyrk has worked at NDR for five years and has been employed on Bentleys for around four decades. He recalls first meeting another of the famous period mechanics, Billy Rockell – who was closely associated with 'Tim' Birkin – when he was working for Stanley Mann in the mid-1970s. Mann's operation was based at Edgware, and Rockell still lived in the same bungalow at Kingsbury as he had done when he was employed by Bentley Motors. 'He worked on the Bentley Team Cars, but when Birkin set up his own team he left the factory to work on the "Blower",' recalls Smyrk. 'Billy was a great guy – very talented – and had a lot of "Bentley skills".'

One of Rockell's tasks at Birkin's Welwyn workshops was acting as supercharger fitter for the single-seater. Others working on this under the direction of Clive Gallop were E.A. Jennings, Walter Whitcombe and Messrs Logan, Newcombe and Browning, the last being the chief chassis fitter.

ABOVE The Paget team's workshop at Welwyn Garden City. *(W.O. Bentley Memorial Foundation)*

LEFT One of the Birkin 'Blowers' being prepared for the 1930 Brooklands Double Twelve. *(W.O. Bentley Memorial Foundation)*

BELOW Bill Rockell joined Birkin's team in 1930 to work on the supercharged cars. *(Colin Smyrk collection)*

CLIENTS' CARS ARE DRIVEN BY THE COMPANY'S STAFF AT OWNER'S RISK.

LONDON OFFICE : 3/5 BURLINGTON GARDENS, W.1   TELEPHONE WELWYN GARDEN 780-1-2.
TELEPHONE : REGENT 3342/3

HENRY BIRKIN & COUPER, LTD.   19/21, BROADWATER ROAD,
AUTOMOBILE, EXPERIMENTAL & PRECISION   WELWYN GARDEN CITY,
ENGINEERS.   HERTS.
DIRECTORS : CAPT. SIR HENRY R. S. BIRKIN, BART.   7th November, 1932.
W. M. COUPER.

TO WHOM IT MAY CONCERN.

This is to certify that W.J. Rockell was employed by us
from November 1929 to November 1932.

We have pleasure in stating that we found him a competent
workman, a good timekeeper and strictly honest.

He is leaving us through no fault of his own and we will
be glad to answer any enquiries concerning him.

Yours faithfully,
for and on behalf of:-
HENRY BIRKIN & COUPER LTD.,

WHILST EVERY REASONABLE PRECAUTION IS TAKEN, THE COMPANY CANNOT ACCEPT LIABILITY FOR
DAMAGE CAUSED BY FIRE TO ANY PROPERTY HELD ON CLIENTS' BEHALF.

LIGHT RELIEF

Neville Minchin, who was closely associated with the automotive industry as a battery supplier, was a regular visitor to Le Mans, and in 1929 took his friend Oliver Lucas of the eponymous electrical concern. That year all the Bentleys, and in particular the 4½-litres, had problems with faulty connectors in the lampholders. After the race it was discovered that the springs in the lampholders carrying the current lost their 'temper' and failed to make contact on heating up. As they cooled down, the springs became active again, made contact and allowed the current to pass once more. Thus the lighting came and went.

Lucas had already lent an electrician to the Bentley team, something that it had never done before. However, a redesign of the lampholder was the only real cure and the unfortunate individual was having a torrid time trying to 'botch' the problem. Barnato, who was understandably unhappy at losing his lights when speeding past the pits, asked Lucas himself if there was anything he could do. The latter approached the harassed electrician, who had no idea that this was his employer, and asked him what was the trouble. Minchin reported that the electrician let fly, telling Lucas to 'run away and don't worry me', although one wonders if this is quite what he said.

Lucas felt that it might not help the situation if he declared his identity and merely commented, 'I, too, know a bit about this stuff, old chap. Come, let me try to help you.' The pair then worked together throughout the night, in Minchin's words 'improvising and patching'. As a result, when dawn broke over La Sarthe all the Bentleys were still running and on their way to total domination of the results.

When Bentley withdrew from racing Billy continued to work on Birkin's cars, including the Maserati at Sir Henry's final race, the Tripoli Grand Prix. In a letter dated January 1985, Rockell stated that he had left Bentley to go to Daimler in 1929 'as I had lost interest' in the company. However, he was shortly to receive a letter from Clive Gallop, by then Birkin's racing manager at Welwyn Garden City. He remembered: 'I joined them in November 1929 and left in November 1931, first working on the engines and then was asked to take on the "Blowers" by Sir Henry Birkin, so I worked on both.'

After leaving Welwyn, Rockell worked on C.F. Turner's long-chassis 'Blower', which was raced on a number of occasions at Brooklands. The Bentley connection continued when he moved on to the service department at Jack Barclay's (he was also to be employed by Harry Rose before the war), before being reunited with former Bentley driver Giulio Ramponi, who was by then chief mechanic for Whitney Straight. This also led to involvement with Dick Seaman's famed voiturette Delage and to a partnership in a garage with Ramponi after the war.

The Bentley interest remained, which was why, as Smyrk says, 'he would continue to pop in and see us at Stanley Mann's. He would even do some part-time work there.' He remembers Rockell, who had acted as Birkin's riding mechanic, as being very methodical.

'He was an engine guy and always used to say that it does not matter which model, the motorcar is "in the valves". If you don't get the valves to seat you've got nothing, and he used to spend hours lapping-in valves. He used to make up little tools that they would use in the factory. Everything was done by hand, nothing by machine.' Such was the dedication of

ABOVE Billy Rockell (left) and Giulio Ramponi in June 1983 presenting the Bentley Drivers Club's floral tribute at the Birkin Blakeney Run, which commemorated the 50th anniversary of Sir Henry's death. *(W.O. Bentley Memorial Foundation)*

LEFT Billy Rockell (left) and Wally Hassan reminisce in later years. *(Neil Davies)*

RIGHT Works mechanic Percy Kemish carrying out what he described as his 'last job' alongside John Carlson, who competed in Brooklands handicap races with YW 5758 in 1931, having purchased the car from Lord Brougham & Vaux. Carlson took the car on a combined business and holiday trip to the Continent and Sweden, offering Kemish the job of a companion who could carry out any servicing necessary. This, said Kemish, 'fortunately was nil'. *(Ian Andrews collection)*

those who worked on the racing Bentleys in W.O.'s era.

'Some say the cars were like trucks,' says Colin, recalling Ettore Bugatti's quote, 'but I can't believe that. These people used to put the cars together by hand and that is why no two are the same. I think the Bentleys are very nice to work on, very simple, very basic, but way ahead of their time. They were doing 16 valves in the 1920s. If you take something like a Lagonda or a Rolls-Royce, they are a lot more involved to work on, a lot more bitty. I think that the Bentley is a very reliable car.

'The reason that Bentley brought in the 4½-litre was that the 3-litre was good but people wanted a little bit more power. W.O. had already done the six-cylinder but people liked the four-cylinder cars. I think they are the best of all. You get a good 4½, then you have something that is really nice.'

CHARLES AMHERST VILLIERS

The man who supercharged the 4½-litre Bentley, Charles Amherst Villiers first came to prominence working on his friend Raymond May's cars, particularly impressing Ettore Bugatti with how he had tuned a pair of Brescia Bugattis. Something of a Renaissance man, it was while working with May that he first became involved with supercharging, blowing the ERA founder's AC and also uprating Humphrey Cook's three-year-old TT Vauxhall in like manner. He additionally designed Malcolm Campbell's first Bluebird but had left the team before it set a new World Land Speed Record on Pendine Sands.

He also supercharged newspaper executive

BELOW Charles Amherst Villiers and Billy Rockell relive old memories. *(W.O. Bentley Memorial Foundation)*

Jack Kruse's Rolls-Royce Phantom 1, and in doing so impressed Sir Henry Birkin when he tried the car – which had been bought by Dorothy Paget – at Brooklands. Consequently, frustrated by the unblown 4½-litre Bentley's uncompetitiveness against a Mercedes SSK, Birkin demanded that the car be supercharged by Villiers. W.O. was unhappy but Barnato agreed that the required 50 production models would be made to enable such a car to go racing.

The agreement with Villiers was far from satisfactory. Amherst was restricted to designing the supercharger and certain ancillaries and to providing the first four units. W.O. was adamant that the supercharger should not clutter up the clean under-bonnet space, and so it was installed sticking out in front of the engine. At the 1929 Motor Show the car was there but there was no reference to Amherst Villiers in the brochure, nor was there, as he thought had been agreed, an embossed acknowledgement on the supercharger itself. Lawyers were summoned, the result being that the brochures were reprinted to say 'The supercharger is the "Amherst Villiers Mk IV",' and a tiny plate was affixed to the front of the unit.

Amherst Villiers was to become involved in the aerospace industry, residing for many years in the USA. When he returned to the UK he assisted BRM, which had earlier been formed by his old friend Mays, with the 1.5-litre engine with which Graham Hill was able to win the 1962 World Championship. Villiers also became a noted artist, one of his subjects being Ian Fleming, the close relevance of this being, as outlined earlier, the author's choice of car for his famed creation, James Bond.

Neil Davies – NDR Limited

ABOVE Neil Davies: 'The 4½-litre is the staple of the market.' *(Ian Wagstaff)*

Neil Davies, a toolmaker by trade, first worked on a Bentley in 1983 when he was with former saloon racer Ivan Dutton. He moved to look after Ed Hubbard's collection of some 40 Bentleys, becoming Hubbard's workshop manager. This led in 1990 to him starting his own business, originally known as Automotive Performance but now NDR Limited, specialising in Cricklewood Bentleys. The original premises, which Davies still owns, was off the St Albans Road in Watford. In 2010 a new premises, also in Watford, was acquired and restored. Up to 30 cars – probably one-third of them 4½-litres – can be on site at any one time. 'We wanted more space and now we have filled it!'

'The 4½-litre is the staple of the market. A "Blower" is a fantastic, fast, aggressive thing. In an ideal world, if doing the Mille Miglia you would drive to Italy in a Speed Six, compete in an event in a short-chassis "Blower", get back in the Speed Six and drive home. The unblown 4½-litre is almost as good as a "Blower" in doing the wiggly stuff and almost as good as a Speed Six at doing the long haul, so it is the bridge in the middle.'

The premises includes an extensive machine shop, trim bay, engine building and a major parts manufacturing operation. The last includes complete 4½-litre engines and superchargers. This means that the company can even make a complete replica, and has done so on a couple of occasions, one being a 4½-litre that was sold to a buyer in South Africa.

Davies owns his own 1927, 'matching numbers' 4½-litre Bentley. 'We've been all over Europe in it; it's the family car.' As far as the most prestigious car the company has worked on, Davies says that has to be the 'single-seater' (see page 123). His company has also restored Speed Six 'Old Number One' back to its two-seater Brooklands form and has restored 'numerous' original 'Blowers'. It says it is the only manufacturer of new 'Blower' engines and Amherst Villiers-pattern superchargers.

BELOW NDR's premises includes an extensive machine shop. *(Ian Wagstaff)*

RIGHT Seen outside NDR, this particular 'Blower' was displayed on the Vanden Plas stand at the 1930 Olympia Motor Show. *(Ian Wagstaff)*

ABOVE The Kingsbury Racing Shop is located on the evocative Bicester Airfield heritage site. Ewen Getley here works on a 1929 4½-litre outside the former engine fitting shop that is now his workshop.
(Ian Wagstaff)

Ewen Getley – Kingsbury Racing Shop

'I grew up with Bentleys and now I restore them,' says Ewen Getley, founder of the Kingsbury Racing Shop. His father had bought a Bentley when a student and he, in turn, learnt to drive in the fields, 'as soon as I could reach the pedals', using the 3-4½-litre car that he currently races.

'Bentley was a very clever engineer and I just find the history and engineering of his cars to be fascinating,' says Getley, himself a qualified engineer.

For many years he worked on Bentleys as a hobby, but for the last decade has turned this into a business. 'I needed a change of direction and somebody phoned me up who was after a crankshaft.' Ewen was able to supply one, which left the customer with the question as to who was going to rebuild his engine. It was a task that Ewen was happy to undertake, which led to the founding of the Kingsbury Racing Shop, named after the shed on the Vanden Plas premises that Bentley used to prepare its competition cars, there being insufficient room at Cricklewood.

The business was originally based in Steeple Aston before moving in 2014 to the nearby Bicester Heritage Centre, 'since when it has become a bit more busy!'

Getley points out that he only has an interest in Cricklewood Bentleys. 'I know it sounds a bit snobbish, but I know nothing about the Derby cars.' For those that admire W.O.'s work, that can be no bad thing. 'I don't want cars in here that I cannot do justice to.'

The main difference in the business that Getley has found over the years is the kind of people who own Bentleys. The price of the cars means that those who now buy them are not

LEFT Most Bentley 4½-litres were never intended for competition. This fixed-head Sportsman Coupe built by Maythorn and Son of Biggleswade is seen outside the Kingsbury Racing Shop.
(Ewen Getley)

necessarily the dyed-in-the-wool enthusiasts who used to own such cars. 'They like to feel a bit special and they like the atmosphere of the place. By being at the Heritage Centre, thousands of people know about the business. I don't have to advertise it.'

The work at Bicester varies considerably. Some cars can be in for major restoration work and can be on the premises for over a year, others may be in for only a couple of days. The ideal is to be working on two or three major projects, a couple of 'slightly more involved service jobs' and a couple of bays open for 'cars coming in for a day or two'. Customers come from as far away as the USA and the Czech Republic.

The premises is the former engine fitting shop – about 3,000ft^2 in size – from when Bicester Airfield was an operational airbase. The Oxfordshire grass runway site dates back to becoming an RFC base in 1916, the succeeding RAF finally leaving in 2004. Flying first took place here in 1911, but it is perhaps best remembered for the fact that the first flight of a Handley Page Halifax started from here.

At the time of writing, Kingsbury had a workforce of three, with Getley looking to double the number. Currently the vastly experienced Neil Spencer and apprentice Matthew Saunders work alongside Ewen. Nearly all the cars that they work on are 4½-litres. 'They are just so lovely,' he reckons, adding that many of the 3-litres also 'turn into 4½-litres. I think they are the best Bentley, an ideal combination of lightness and power.' Getley reckons that they are probably driven mostly these days because they are ideal for historic rallies. He also points out the commonality of external parts with the 3-litre.

Ewen has raced and hill climbed his 3-4½-litre extensively. Successes have included the VSCC's Lycett Trophy (given to the driver gaining the most points during the season driving an Edwardian or Vintage car). 'My greatest triumphs are when I beat heavily modified specials.'

RIGHT A recreation of a 'bobtail' 4½-litre Bentley is under way at Vintage Bentley Heritage.
(Ian Wagstaff)

William Medcalf – Vintage Bentley Heritage

William Medcalf runs three companies under the umbrella of 'Vintage Bentley Heritage' which include sales, parts and a substantial workshop. 'So,' says Medcalf, 'we have a closed loop from 1922 to 1932. If anyone comes through the door with a dream to win an event, drive around the world or something even more daring in a vintage Bentley, then we can assist, from sourcing the car to running it. Total support and service is absolutely what we do.'

Around 30 vintage Bentleys are on site at any one time, all with a deadline to meet.

ABOVE Modern technology sits side-by-side with vintage cars at Vintage Bentley Heritage. *(Ian Wagstaff)*

'Being able to deliver to these global events drives the company forward in a positive way.' The 4½-litres feature quite heavily as they are a model of choice, and account for around a dozen of the cars being worked on.

Medcalf's father Bill, a toolmaker by trade, owned a 3-4½-litre Bentley. 'When I was just five years old, my father's idea of a family holiday was 28,000 miles around America in nine months! Bentleys, travelling the world and meeting new cultures is what I enjoy most.' His father put skills into the hands of his son and by the time he had left school Medcalf Junior had already restored his first car (a Morris Minor). He swiftly moved on to Bentleys, working in the family yard in Edmonton, North London. That was over two decades ago. Seventeen years later the family yard was swamped with Bentleys, and a new 1½-acre site – a former main dealership – in West Sussex ('on the road from Brooklands to Goodwood') was found and the businesses relocated.

By the end of 2016 the companies had a combined staff of 22, including 'a qualified and experienced engineer' heading up the manufacturing business (Benchmark Precision Engineering). With a fully equipped machine shop and a SolidWorks CAD department and CNC capability the business now holds the largest stock of parts in the world. A turning centre is planned for the near future, 'which will give us complete control in-house to manufacture anything we need'.

In partnership with Surrey University, the company is also studying new ways 'to develop

our parts to a new level'. The company was planning for the future at the time of writing, already embracing modern technologies such as scanning and 3D printing. The codification of process and assembly was in full swing.

An 'experienced racing mechanic' heads up the workshop (William Medcalf Limited). An engine building room with seven units 'in build' is led by engine builder Jamie Broom, who has been working on Bentley power units for just under four decades. There is an in-house engine dyno where every unit built is run in for eight to ten hours before being maxed out. Mark Hopkins in the trim shop also has 40 years' experience of his trade, specifically with Bentleys.

'I think it is a responsibility to secure the tooling and the specialist knowledge from the past and present in one place in order to enjoy it in the future.'

Chapter Five

The owner's view

With so many Bentley 4½-litre cars still in existence, it is inevitable that a number of them are still used in competition. Current owners range from those like Martin Overington, who truly believes his car to be a thing that should race, to Bentley Motors itself, which now ensures perhaps the most noted of all 'Blowers' can still be admired. A vibrant industry has grown up to support them.

OPPOSITE 'It is the model of choice for many people who go rallying.' – William Medcalf, Vintage Bentley Heritage. *(Andrea Seed)*

ABOVE The ex-Birkin single-seater was sold at auction for £5.2 million in 2012. *(W.O. Bentley Memorial Foundation)*

BELOW XV 1200, seen here following a 3-litre Bentley past the Brooklands test hill, was sold at Bonhams' Goodwood auction in 2013 for £785,000. *(Ian Wagstaff)*

Bentley 4½ litre values

Bentley historian Claire Hay has pointed out that a Vanden Plas sports-bodied Bentley 4½-litre is not a rare car, with about half of those built still surviving; but, as William Medcalf adds, we are dealing with a finite market. He reckons that wherever he drives a Bentley in the world, 'one of the top three questions that people ask is "What's it worth?" After a while I realised that people generally have no idea, which is great! A funny old car receives a much warmer welcome than a modern play station car, which everyone knows what you paid for it.'

This book is specifically concerned with the 4½-litre as a racing car, and while those that raced in period really are limited in number and would be very expensive if they came on the market, there is little reason why any of the others still extant could not be prepared for use in a 21st-century race or rally.

The value of Bentley 4½-litres varies enormously, from £450,000 for a non-matching numbers, replica-bodied, 'not particularly nice' car, to £1 million and perhaps just over for a matching numbers, original body but 'run-of-the-mill' one; something coach-built, a Drop Head or a Saloon, could cost even more. Above this, there are still the team cars where, if one were to become available, we would be into the world of the ultra rare and the multiple millions of pounds that can be asked for such vehicles. 'As soon as you says the words "Le Mans" or "Brooklands" then you have kicked off into another league,' observes Medcalf. Any 'Blower' worth its salt is going to fetch over £3 million. An original-bodied one or one with significant history could be nearer £4–£5 million. As an example, the ex-Birkin 'single-seater', which had competed at Le Mans in its original tourer guise, is known to have been sold for £5.2 million at auction in 2012, and the buyer admitted he would have paid double!

Originality is now key with, says Neil Davies, 'continuous history now more important than matching numbers'. Medcalf concurs: 'It is so dependent on continuous history, on ownership

history. Their worth is very much on an individual basis.'

Potential buyers need to know that the car has not been, as Ewen Getley puts it, 'mucked about with'. Barn finds are ideal because they are demonstrably original cars. Having said this, Neil Davies remarks that a car is more likely to be original because there was nothing remarkable or successful about it and it has been just 'parked' for many years. He compares this to UU 44, a car built-up by 'Rusty' Russ-Turner in the 1950s – a complete 'bitza' as he describes it. Included in this car was the four-seater Vanden Plas body from what became the single-seater, an original 4½-litre chassis and a supercharged engine that Russ-Turner built from spares. 'It had all original Bentley bits, and what a lovely car,' Davies observes. 'It was much more exciting than some boring old Vanden Plas long-wing tourer that happens to have survived probably because it broke down in 1939.' Davies leaves you in no doubt as to which car he would prefer, even if is not 'original', adding that if you do own a particularly low-mileage, excellent condition example there is no way in which you are going to risk it in competition.

Money does not necessarily buy opportunity. Some of the 4½-litres are locked away in family ownership where money is irrelevant. 'You can like the car as much as you want and offer as much as you want but if they don't want to sell it, they don't want to sell it,' says Medcalf. 'Cars are often part of the family.'

Obtaining spare parts

Unfortunately nearly all the racing drawings were destroyed when the company was sold to Rolls-Royce, but most of the parts were simply carried over on to the road cars. The availability of parts is, indeed, very good. The major reason for this is the sheer number of vintage Bentleys that still exist. They are not rare cars, just extremely desirable ones. As one of its members admits, the vintage Bentley business is a 'cottage industry' and those involved know where to easily source a component, assuming that they do not manufacture it themselves.

Companies such as the Kingsbury Racing Shop, NDR and Vintage Bentley Heritage

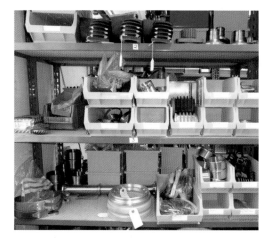

LEFT **Parts in stock at NDR...** (Ian Wagstaff)

LEFT **...and at Vintage Bentley Heritage.** (Ian Wagstaff)

will, indeed, make many of the parts needed themselves. Otherwise, as Kingsbury's Ewen Getley observes, 'I can pretty much lay my hands on anything required within a few days.' As Medcalf points out, there is an extensive supply chain with 'a network of blacksmiths

BELOW **Gasket set for a 4½-litre Bentley.** (Ian Wagstaff)

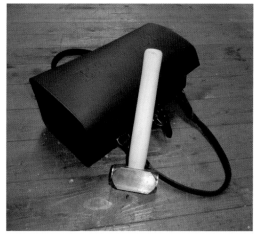

and old toolmakers' that can support major operations such as the above. However, 'it is harder to get modern companies to understand what we want, so we are doing more and more in-house,' says Getley.

Neil Davies points out that when he first started working on Bentleys, the only person for spare parts was Donald Day, who is still in operation. Since then the market has evolved and while there are a number of sources, the main two are Davies' own NDR and Medcalf's operation, both of which are profiled in chapter four. 'Having the parts on the shelf is absolutely key,' says Medcalf. He believes that it is also important to manufacture parts in the original style and to the original design. 'It might be cheaper to manufacture them in a more economical way but that is just devaluing the brand.'

Such is the nature of the marque that specialist equipment is also available, in addition to conventional parts. William Medcalf, for example, will supply a bespoke tool kit which

includes King Dick spanners, as would have originally been supplied, and a copper wheel hammer, which is an exact copy of the original. 'We live in a world of detail and we find that our clients really appreciate this and are happy to pay for it.'

It should also be noted that the Bentley Drivers Club operates The Vintage Bentley Spares Scheme, which is organised and run from its Wroxton headquarters for members.

Insurance

When it comes to insuring a vintage Bentley 4½-litre, there are lots of different factors to take into account, and it is important that the risk is placed with an insurance company that understands the complexities involved with insuring such a unique vehicle. There are four types of insurance cover available, which allow for the car to be used on the road and garaged by the owner when not in use, cover for storage and transit between circuits, cover for racing while on track and for rallying, beyond Europe and including competitive timed rallying.

Standard classic car insurance policies may be suitable for road use, but choose your insurer wisely and make sure the policy covers you for what you need. Some policies come with European travel, breakdown cover and agreed valuation included. The last is essential for a car such as a pre-war Bentley, where originality and history can account for huge fluctuations in the value of a car. Furthermore, check your policy allows the owner to choose their repairer should damage rectification be

LEFT A pair of 4½-litres at the Shuttleworth 'Race Day' in October 2016. Nearest to the camera is Jonathan White's 1930 model, which was rebuilt in the 1930s. Furthest away is Richard Holland's 1928 short-chassis example, with Bristol Aviation aluminium lightweight bodywork, that was successfully raced post-war by Douglas Wilson-Spratt. *(Ian Wagstaff)*

required. This is essential if the provenance of an important Bentley is to be maintained. The biggest risks against this policy are fire and road accident, although theft of classic vehicles is on the rise. In the event of a total loss, the owner must make sure their insurance covers the purchase of a similar replacement vehicle.

Specialist marine insurance is available for damage only or for total loss – *ie* if the car were being shipped abroad for a race and the ship sank (this happened to one Bentley), the insurance would pay out. The vehicle should be covered for its full market value so a replacement could be purchased in the event of a total loss. The other variation of this policy is Accidental Damage, Fire and Theft. With this, no cover is provided while the car is under its own power. A feature of the policy offered by Hagerty International, the classic car and bike insurance specialists, is that cover is also provided when the car is in transit between locations such as racetracks and garages that specialise in motor sport preparation. If the vehicle is travelling outside the UK or Europe, full details of the journey should be supplied, as a separate policy may be required.

The 'On Track' insurance tends to be an expensive policy, given the risk exposure arising from racing a vehicle on a circuit in a competition. Such cover will usually require the policyholder to accept a high 'excess', this being the amount that the policyholder must pay in the case of a claim against the insurance. The 'excess' would be somewhere in the region of 15% to 20% of the vehicle value and would allow for most bumps and

scrapes endured during competitive motor sport. Underwriters tend to offer lower rates for drivers who agree to accept even higher levels of 'excess'. The cover may often exclude accidents arising from engine failure or from burst tyres, and the detail should always be reviewed before purchase.

ABOVE Sati Lall's 1930 'Blower' arrives at one of its spiritual homes, Brooklands, in early 2017… *(Ian Wagstaff)*

LEFT …as does Piers Wilson's 1928 4½-litre. *(Ian Wagstaff)*

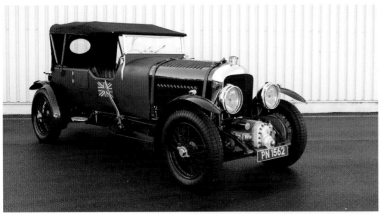

LEFT Historic Competition Services offers race and rally preparation for Bentley 4½-litres in Wommelgem, Belgium. A 1928 supercharged example of such a car could be found on the company's stand at the 2016 Interclassics Show in Brussels. This had been disassembled in 1961, the engine being installed elsewhere. It was subsequently rebuilt by Stanley Mann and the missing engine replaced by Neil Davies. *(Wim Van Roy)*

Maintenance

Vintage Bentleys require very little maintenance as they were designed to be durable cars. On a day-to-day basis, the Bentley 4½-litre is amazingly bulletproof. This is why they were so successful over 24 hours at Le Mans. Bentley 4½-litres use twin magnetos, so if a magneto packs up it is still possible to continue driving down the road. There is also no head gasket, so there will be no head gasket failure.

Typical maintenance involves the lubrication of the 32 oil nipples in varying order of importance, from king-pins every 500 miles to hand brake once a year. It is noted that the use of heavy oil is proscribed and under no circumstances is grease to be used anywhere. Given the high use of some of these Bentleys a routine of 'spanner checking' is adopted, even daily, on long-distance events to ensure the security of components from the rigours of adventure. Oil is cheaper than metal (at the time of writing) so frequent oil changes are recommended. 'A wise owner insists on cleaning his car, therefore he knows his car,' says William Medcalf.

There is much about the car that is allied to aircraft engineering, thanks to W.O.'s work on rotary engines during the Great War. That is significant; engine failure in a car may be inconsequential, but engine failure in a Sopwith 7.F1 Snipe above the trenches could so easily be fatal. Towards the end of the war, Bentley's aircraft engines were doing something like 70 hours between overhauls; the Clergets from which his BR.1 and BR.2, with their aluminium pistons, were developed had needed 15 hours.

The Bentley Drivers Club has been publishing its *Technical Facts of the Vintage Bentley* since 1955 and is now on its fifth edition.

Competition opportunities

The opportunities for a Bentley 4½-litre owner to enter competitions are, observes William Medcalf, endless. 'I believe the best way to see a Bentley 4½-litre is coming sideways through a chicane,' he says. Racing for such cars in the years just after the Second World War tended to be at Vintage Sports Car Club and Bentley Drivers Club meetings. Cars were regularly modified with no thought to maintaining originality. The races were, and still are, short, perhaps ten-lap events for club cups. At a typical BDC meeting an owner can enter more than one race, but the cars that were chopped about to win in the 1950s and 1960s have often been restored to their original state, with the ability to cover ten laps of the Silverstone short circuit no longer considered to be of prime importance.

Racing opportunities have grown since the early days of the VSCC and BDC meeting with such as those offered by Duncan Wiltshire's Motor Racing Legends series, Wiltshire being on the BDC's main board. In recent years there have been suitable races appearing on the cards at such events as the Goodwood Revival,

Silverstone and the Le Mans Classic, as well as at such iconic tracks as Spa-Francorchamps, Zandvoort and the historic hill climb at Ollon Villars in Switzerland, while a 4½-litre is eligible for the Mille Miglia, which, strictly speaking, is no longer a race.

It is Medcalf's contention that 4½-litres were not, though, designed for short races. W.O. intended them for endurance events, often on far from smooth surfaces. The popular historic navigational and long-distance rallies, pioneered by Philip Young, are perhaps the

ABOVE The opportunities to compete with a Bentley 4½-litre have been said to be 'endless'. *(Ian Wagstaff)*

Bentley Drivers Club

Silverstone Race Meeting · Saturday 28 August 1971

Programme 15p

BENTLEY DRIVERS CLUB MEETING

SPONSORED BY W.D. & H.O. WILLS

PRICE 2/-

SILVERSTONE
SATURDAY 20th AUGUST

ABOVE Although 4½-litre Bentleys have raced at Silverstone for many years, the circuit hardly provides a classic backdrop. *(Ian Wagstaff)*

BELOW Bentley 4½-litres were raced regularly at club events during the 1950s and 1960s. In those days a 'track side' photographer's pass could mean just that. As a filmmaker, driver Bill Mason must have appreciated this photographer's determination. *(Nick Mason collection)*

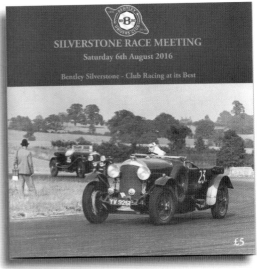

nearest to those. They have provided new opportunities for such cars and there are now four major companies organising such events: the Endurance Rally Association, Rally Round, HERO and Bespoke Rallies. 'The great thing with Bentleys is that when you have finished the day's rallying, you can spend the evening in the bar, rather than under the car.' The reliable and relatively comfortable Bentley 4½-litre is surely ideal for an event such as the Peking–Paris. The 4½ is a very balanced and driveable car and there is plenty of room in the back for luggage and spares. It is equally at home on circuit work and on loose gravel stages. It can also cope with long distances. Medcalf has won more than anyone in such events as the Peking–Paris, Flying Scotsman and Alpine Trial. 'These events are quite serious and full-on and a 4½-litre is a good all-rounder to use. That is why it is the model of choice for many people who now go rallying.'

The Endurance Rally Association is perhaps responsible for some of the best known of this type of event, with, at the time of writing, the next Peking to Paris Challenge due to take place in 2019. More frequent are the Flying Scotsman, the 2017 edition of which will finish at Gleneagles; the Blue Train Challenge, described as a five-day motoring adventure from Deauville to Cannes; and the Alpine Trial, due to take place next in 2018. Other rallies under the ERA banner have been run in places such as South America, Africa and the Baltic States. Bespoke Rallies is another that will take participants far afield, including South America and the Himalayas. Rally

ABOVE The number of 4½-litres racing in BDC events may have shrunk, with Guy Northam's standard version the only one competing at the club's 2016 Silverstone meeting. *(Ian Wagstaff)*

ABOVE Bentley 4½-litres have been regular competitors at the VSCC's Pomeroy Trophy. D.J. Brewster briefly owned this one (seen here at the 1966 event on the old start/finish straight at Silverstone) in late 1965 and early 1966 before selling it to A.E. Talby that April. *(Ian Wagstaff)*

LEFT Vintage sports cars were on the card at the Goodwood Revival in 2015. Martin Overington drove with 4½-litre customary verve. *(Jochen Van Caulwenberge)*

LEFT Following the successful Glen Kidston Trophy of 2015, vintage cars such as 4½-litre Bentleys were invited to again take part in the 2017 Silverstone Classic. Jochen Ernst took part in the first of these with the 'Blower' that was displayed on the Vanden Plas stand at the 1930 Motor Show. *(Courtesy Silverstone Classic)*

ABOVE Jochen Ernst's 'Blower' turns into Abbey Corner during the 2015 Glen Kidston Trophy. *(Jakob Ebrey)*

RIGHT There are still opportunities for Bentley 4½-litres to race at Le Mans. One such was the race run by Duncan Wiltshire's Motor Racing Legends on the morning of the 2005 24 Hours. Here Chris Guest's unblown example races towards the Dunlop Bridge. *(Ian Wagstaff)*

RIGHT The Peking–Paris is a true test of resilience for the Bentley 4½-litre. Keith and Norah Ashworth's William Medcalf-prepared version, which has competed on many such events, provides proof. *(Andrea Seed)*

Round has been to Burma and Bhutan and is also responsible for events starting in Paris and heading for major European cities. HERO events tend to be nearer home and include the Royal Automobile Club 1,000 Mile Trial.

These event companies are responsible for building a multi-million pound industry, with two major logistics companies existing to move cars round from event to event. Their reliability has ensured that Bentley 4½-litres are often to the fore of the results, while they will be outclassed in short races. 'On some events you can expect half the field to be vintage Bentleys,' remarks Medcalf.

Do not expect to win when it comes to shorter racing events. 'We tend to be outclassed,' says Getley. 'There has been so much development of other cars and we are still running what are essentially four-seat tourers. They are big, one-and-a-half-ton cars. A Bugatti is an 850-kilo car and it's small. You do not have to carry out much development to a Bugatti to always beat a Bentley. What you do get with a Bentley is a most versatile car; you can just get in, start it and drive. Bugattis don't work on Thursdays but Bentleys work every day! I can drive a Bentley to a meeting and win a race or rally; I can take three friends to the pub or drive to Monaco. There are not many cars that will do all these things. They may not be the best car for trialling, the most comfortable in which to travel to Monte Carlo

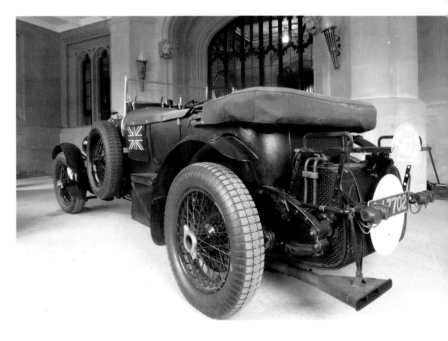

ABOVE Louise Carledge and Max Stephenson hit the ford in their 1930 4½-litre during the 7th Flying Scotsman in 2015. *(Tony Large)*

ABOVE RIGHT The early laps of the BRC Portimão 24 Hours were raced hood-up, as in period. This is Katrina Kyvalova's 1928 4½-litre. *(Gerard Brown)*

BELOW Le Mans-style pits were recreated at Portimão for the BRC 24 Hours. Gerard Lunn's 1929 4½-litre Bentley poses in front of them. *(Gerard Brown)*

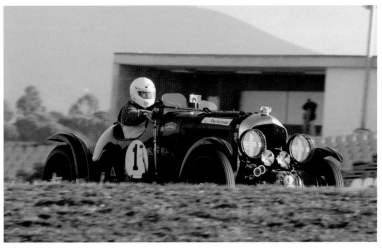

or the fastest car on the circuit, but they give a decent account of themselves in all of those things. Take the late, great Stanley Mann. He would drive everywhere in one of his cars. He would never take a trailer anywhere.'

When it comes to current drivers Martin Overington is 'the man. He can throw that car around the circuit with the most amazing speed,' says Getley. Guy Northam is another regular race competitor in a standard 4½-litre. However, it may be that, as Medcalf sadly predicts, the modern short circuit racing days will soon be over for the 4½-litre. At the BDC's 2016 August meeting Northam was the only person to compete with such a car.

That is as may be, but BDC competitions captain Mike Haig points out the variety still available to the 4½-litre owner wanting to compete on the smaller scale. In addition to race meetings, there are also sprints and hill climbs that can be particularly suitable. The BDC itself runs an annual sprint at the industry research track, MIRA, while the Benjafield Racing Club holds a one-lap sprint at Goodwood. The VSCC also holds sprints and hill climbs. 'We will never turn our back on competition,' says BDC chairman Ron Warmington.

'Bentley 4½-litres are also welcome at the Wiscombe Park, Loton Park, Bo'ness hill climbs, the Brighton Speed Trials and a sprint meeting at Castle Combe,' says Haig. 'And even the old Rest and Be Thankful hill climb in Scotland is still used for an event, although it can no longer be timed.'

LEFT The BRC 24 Hours was not the first time that Bentleys had raced at Portimão. This is the 4½-litre 'Blower' of Nigel Batchelor at the Algarve Historic Festival in 2010. *(Ian Wagstaff)*

The future may be in recreations of historic long-distance races. In 2014, in celebration of Bentley's first victory at Le Mans, the Benjafield's Racing Club ran a 24-hour race on the Portimão circuit in Portugal. Included in the 21-strong entry of pre-war cars were Bentley 4½-litres from Georg Weidmann, Katrina Kyvalova, Christopher Lunn, Christian Schenk and Jean-Pierre Mueller. The 4½-litre Pacey-Hassan also acted as the pace car. Hoods were up for the first 20 laps and the pits were recreated in 1920s Le Mans style. 'The Bentleys came alive,' recalled Medcalf, who as the BRC's competitions captain pioneered the idea. The plan is that this will be followed in 2017 by the Benjafield's 500-mile race at Spain's Ascari circuit in the style of the Brooklands event won in 1929 by a 4½-litre. This, it is hoped, will be followed by a Double Twelve and then another 24-hour. Pre-war cars, particularly Bentleys, are totally suited for such long-distance events.

Restored and preserved examples

Attend any event involving vintage cars – from Kop Hill to Windsor Castle – and the chances are there will be 4½-litre Bentleys present. With so many having been built in period, these will come from a mix that can be divided into normally aspirated and supercharged, or even examples of the former that have been 'blown' subsequently.

The cars may be anything from a pukka team car to a production model on which a replica of a Vanden Plas Le Mans body has replaced that of a once thought more mundane (if such a word can be used in this context) saloon. The fact is that Bentley never built a complete car, with the customer sourcing the bodywork from such coachbuilders as Vanden Plas, Gurney Nutting or Maythorn. Thus, although over the years many bodies have been changed, that is not to say these are not original cars.

It may be, though, that what you are looking at was driven by Sir Henry Birkin himself and, if so, is a truly historic artefact. This section covers a varied selection of Bentley 4½-litres still in use, starting with one of arguably the most famous of them all.

UU 5872 – Bentley Motors

Bentley acquired UU 5872, the Birkin Blower No 2 Team Car, from Victor Gauntlet at the turn of the century. Bentley Brand Ambassador Richard Charlesworth had said to him on many an occasion that should he ever want to sell, the company would be interested. 'He told me that he never would, but then for various reasons the car was flushed out. I was in London in the

ABOVE The short-chassis 4½-litre of Christian Hore and Ben Cussons on the 2016 Royal Automobile Club 1,000-Mile Trial. *(Tony Large)*

BELOW The 1929 4½-litre of Ireland's Andrew Bailey and Philippa Spiller out in the wilds on the 2015 Flying Scotsman. *(Tony Large)*

pouring rain at the time when the phone rang. I went under the canopy of a shop to take the call. It was Victor, who said, "The car's in play."' There was already a bid from America and the money was on its way, but if Bentley could get the required amount into his bank that day, the company could have it. 'We made it happen,' recalls Charlesworth. As he points out, it is a 'hugely important car', having been the very mount that Birkin used to harass Caracciola at Le Mans in 1930. 'It's arguably the most valuable Bentley in the world,' he claims.

The car had undergone a modest restoration in the 1960s when it was owned by Stanley Sears. 'All we have done since is to mechanically keep it in good order, changing as little as possible, certainly not the important bits.'

The car is used regularly. Since becoming owned by Bentley, it has competed on the modern Mille Miglia a number of times. (This actual car was entered for the event in 1930 but failed to start.) 'It's been around the world. We've had it in the Middle East, in the United States. It regularly travels to the Le Mans 24 Hours, enabling modern Bentley owners to experience it as a passenger.'

After Bentley's victory at Le Mans in 2003 it took part in the impromptu victory parade on the Champs-Élysées. The winning car took the lead, driven on this occasion by Derek Bell. Behind came two "Blowers" with the winning trio of Tom Kristensen, Rinaldo Capello and Guy Smith perched in the back of UU 5872, which

was being driven by then Bentley chairman Dr Franz-Josef Paefgen.

'It is a living part of Bentley history that we want to keep living. We don't want to stick it in a glass cage surrounded by cotton wool balls. We treat it carefully, but we use it,' says Charlesworth.

Understandably, the number of those privileged to drive the car is limited. Charlesworth is one, as is the current Bentley chairman Wolfgang Dürheimer plus just a few others. Two of these are the pair responsible for its maintenance, Keith Downey and Vito Bilotta. To the above can be added a Le Mans winner from the modern era, Derek Bell, sharing the driving with Charlesworth on the Ennstal Classic. In addition to participating on the event itself, Bell drove it on the road to the venue, with his wife Misty and son Sebastian, in order to get used to the car.

Undoubtedly, the general public has a fascination for the blown 4½-litre Bentley. When Birkin introduced it, it clearly had much more horsepower, and Birkin was a charismatic individual. The British looked at what he had done against Caracciola in the Mercedes at Le Mans and thought, 'That is just fantastic.' Birkin was not just racing for Bentley; he was racing for King and Country. Thus the 'Blower' Bentley entered into the consciousness of the British public from that day on. Having said that, if you look at what W.O. said regarding why the company went bust, one of the three reasons cited was the failure of the blown car. It was untested and therefore unreliable. Also, when compared to the unblown car, the performance uplift of the 'Factory 50' versions, which produced substantially less power than Birkin's Team Cars, was relatively modest and their fuel consumption markedly worse.

YW 5758 – Dr Ian Andrews

Although a 'Blower' Bentley never won a major endurance race, two of the conventional cars did, YW 5758 being one of them. It was with this car that Frank Clement and Jack Barclay came first in the 1929 Brooklands 500-mile race. Although used as a team car, it was, like all other cars entered by the factory at this time, privately owned, in this case by Humphrey Cook who financed the ERA voiturette single-seaters. Before being purchased by the current

BELOW Five times Le Mans winner Derek Bell and Bentley ambassador Richard Charlesworth with UU 5872 on the 2016 Ennstal Classic.
(Ennstal Classic archive)

owner the car was raced year in year out at almost every Bentley Drivers Club Silverstone meeting since the inception of the club. It was competitively driven by its previous owners Harry Rose and his daughter Ann Shoosmith over a 30-year period of ownership.

YW 5758 is a significant example of the breed. Indeed, there is no other original-bodied Bentley in existence that has a better racing history. The current owner, Dr Ian Andrews, has owned the car for the best part of 20 years. He recalls: 'I looked at a number of Bentleys over a two-year period and spent a considerable amount of time researching the marque, making every attempt to acquire a vintage Bentley that suited my requirements. During this time I came close to purchasing a "blown" 4½-litre, but when I first saw the car that I now have I realised immediately that my search had ended. Two things were very apparent. Firstly, the car looked very tired, by which I mean the Bentley had been raced continuously by its previous owners and was in need of some TLC – indeed, its racing history from the 1920s and early 1930s is engraved on the radiator. Secondly, this Bentley has considerable originality. It has its original chassis number, original engine and gearbox and, above all, its original Vanden Plas coachwork.

'The racing history of this Bentley has been well documented both in film and in print. Indeed, in a book by Elizabeth Nagle called *The Other Bentley Boys*, which in my opinion is probably one of the best books that has ever been written on the vintage Bentley, Wally Hassan noted that "YW" was a particularly fast car … we really went to town on it … the Bentley lapping Brooklands at almost 110mph to win the 500 Miles race in 1929.

'Indeed, there are only two original-bodied Bentleys in existence that have won major Blue Riband races. One is "Old Number Two" Speed Six and the other one is YW 5758. Although I am not particularly interested in concours events, YW won a major FIVA award for originality at Parc Bagatelle a number of years ago and was the highest-placed team car at Pebble Beach in 2009 when Bentley Motors attended the

LEFT Reflected glory. YW 5758's results are engraved either side of the radiator cap. *(Ian Wagstaff)*

BELOW Dr Ian Andrews took the 1929 BRDC 500-mile winner back to Brooklands in early 2017. *(Ian Wagstaff)*

RIGHT A painting of YW 5758 by an unknown artist. *(Courtesy Dr Ian Andrews)*

concours event to celebrate its 90th Anniversary. It is, however, a real pleasure for me to take the Bentley back to the race tracks where its provenance was crafted, namely at the racing circuits of Newtownards in Northern Ireland, Phoenix Park in Dublin, Brooklands and Le Mans. I also feel that it is particularly important to both celebrate and help perpetuate the marque and ensure that the contribution the racing Bentley made to the history of motor racing continues to be recognised.

'Newtownards is very much the same today as it was back in 1928. Humphrey Cook, the original owner of "YW", raced in the inaugural TT in 1928 and W.O. Bentley was alongside Tim Birkin in his "Blower" in 1929. The circuit was founded upon public roads, so everyone still has the opportunity to drive on the 13.5-mile track. Every five years I and many other vintage Bentley owners return to Newtownards to commemorate the TT races. The interest here continues to be exceptional.

'Similarly, in 1929, Phoenix Park, Dublin, staged the inaugural Irish International Grand Prix, a race that was dominated by Bentley, the marque taking four of the first five places. Humphrey Cook was again a member of this winning team. I have been fortunate enough to have participated in one or two commemorative races at the Park and its configuration is little changed today. It is also worth noting that whenever there is a discussion about the racing Bentley, Brooklands and Le Mans are often used to illustrate the point being made. However, it is also true to say that the two principal racing circuits in Ireland were equally significant and attracted the finest international drivers of the day.

'Nonetheless, Brooklands is the true spiritual home of the racing Bentley. "YW" raced at the circuit on numerous occasions – its most famous accolade was winning the 500-miles race there in 1929, which was also the first BRDC race to be held. It has been noted in another chapter just how significant Brooklands became to the development of the racing Bentley and in turn how developmental work conducted at Weybridge significantly assisted Bentley Motors in dominating Le Mans during the 1920s. I continue to take the car back to Brooklands for all sorts of historical events and it is a real privilege to be able to do so.

'There is perhaps little I can add to the legend that is Le Mans suffice to say that I have taken the car back to the circuit on a number of occasions. Like Brooklands, Le Mans never loses its magic for me. In 1929 "YW" was in second place after 12 hours of racing, only for the ballast being carried to dislodge and foul the brake rods. The car was to finish fourth.

'While I am fortunate enough to have a racing Bentley I have also derived a huge amount of satisfaction from meeting a myriad of fascinating enthusiasts along the way. Be it an owner of a Morris Minor, Maserati, Mercedes Benz or Mini, all these owners similarly take immense pleasure in the cars that they have. Using these cars gives thousands of like-minded individuals, including myself, enormous pleasure in being able to see them on the road, where they belong. I equally use my Bentley, but having written and read an awful lot about the Bentley marque one thing is absolutely certain – I am not really a Bentley owner, rather, I am simply a custodian.'

GY 3905 – National Motor Museum

Bill Boddy, the opinionated editor of *Motor Sport* magazine, did not like it. As far as he was concerned, the car was a fraud, and Edward, Lord Montagu, had jaundiced the market by paying a high price for it. True, despite its appearance it was not a Paget Team 'Blower' Car. Indeed, it had started life as anything but, with a Vanden Plas coupé body with dickie seat, but it was an all-matching numbers chassis from the batch of 50 supercharged 4½-litre cars manufactured by Bentley and, 'genuine' as such. There was also the fact that rebuilt as a replica of Birkin's car, it arguably had greater appeal for visitors to Montagu's National Motor Museum.

By the late 1960s the car had become virtually derelict. Elmdown Restoration rebuilt it to look like one of the Paget cars with replica body, shortened chassis, fibreglass mudguards and sealed beam headlight unit inside the original headlight frames. It had originally been fitted with a black Vanden Plas sportsman's coupé body. The museum's manager Doug Hill admits that it has been a much-criticised car, 'because it is trying to look like something that

it was not originally, but you cannot detract that it is an original-chassis, original running gear "Blower" Bentley.'

In the early 1970s the then Lord Montagu purchased the car at auction for £16,500 and donated it to the new National Motor Museum Trust. 'When we acquired it there were a number of things wrong with it. It needed to be used and settled down. However, for a number of years this just did not happen. The engine was "rattley" and it was just not a nice car. It was a shame that we had such a nice car that we did not enjoy using. In 1992 Hill and Montagu took it on a *voiture ancienne* Monaco Rally, 'a tour with regularity stages. It was not particularly arduous, but we were up in the Alps when it knocked a big end out.'

As a result the engine was stripped out by a Bentley specialist. A Phoenix steel billet crankshaft was fitted, as was a full-flow oil filter and various other components. (The museum also retained the original parts.) The car now enjoyed a very healthy oil pressure. To run the engine in, Hill drove it from Beaulieu to Aberdeen to compete in a sprint meeting at the Grampian Transport Museum. It was then driven 'pretty much daily' and again entered for the retrospective Monte Carlo event, which it won. The rally started in Baden Baden, with Hill initially driving it from Beaulieu to Stuttgart in one day.

The car is not particularly fast because of a low-ratio back axle – 2,500 revs equate to 64mph on the road – 'but it will sit there all day'. Despite the lack of a speedometer Hill is well aware that it will do over 100mph, 'as the

Scottish police told me one night'. (He now uses a GPS speedometer.)

Hill reckons that he has driven the car from Beaulieu to Monaco on at least half a dozen occasions. Since 1994, in excess of 66,000 miles have been 'clocked'.

One of the Beaulieu Bentley's many appearances was at the Kop Hill revival meeting in 2013 where the supercharger failed (although one of the authors was in the car at the time, he points out it was not his fault as he was in the front passenger seat). The failure was caused by one of the two fibre drive couplings becoming very hard and not taking any of the flex out of the drive. Subsequently the whole of the drive system was chattering and 'just wore itself out'. The supercharger was subsequently rebuilt and the rotors lightened.

ABOVE The National Motor Museum's 4½-litre *in situ* **at Beaulieu.** *(Ian Wagstaff)*

BELOW Kop Hill awaits GY 3905. *(Ian Wagstaff)*

The magneto on the exhaust side tends to overheat despite robust heat shields, and it often drops on to one magneto. At night you can see the exhaust glowing cherry red. 'In hot weather, it starts getting flustered and the mixture starts to change. It normally richens up and you have to be very careful that you do not over-weaken it.'

The car now runs on an alternator, fitted by Neil Davies, and has had a Kenlowe fan fitted. Other than that, it runs as original. 'It has become a bit of an old friend,' observes Hill. 'We have about 20 cars in the collection which are "on the button" and it is one of the most iconic of these. It does not have to be transported. If we have film or promotional work to do we are likely to pick on this car. We obviously have to decide if an event is suitable for the vehicle. We don't just use it willy-nilly, but it is not wrapped in cotton wool. It does not matter if it goes out in the wet. In fact, it runs so much better when it's raining, it enjoys the damp air.'

Although he gave the Bentley to the Trust, it remained, in effect, very much Edward Montagu's car and he would often call Hill to tell him that he wanted to take it out. 'He did tell me that he wanted to go across India in it, but I told him that it wasn't suitable.' However, in 1997 Hill started the Peking–Paris in a 1915 Vauxhall, which failed in Mongolia and he finished the event with the 'Blower' Bentley, taking it to Rimini, where he rejoined his fellow contestants.

GP 8242 – Martin Overington

It has been said that Martin Overington is the last person to properly race a Bentley 4½-litre. Such is the nature of these historic cars that they are more likely to be simply driven rather than really raced when entered in competition.

'It was a childhood dream for me,' he says. Even at the age of five, Overington had asked his father, John, the identity of a car, to be told that it was a Bentley 'Blower' and that 'it fires every other lamp post'. By the time he was in his mid-40s his childhood dreams had come to fruition, and he purchased a normally aspirated 4½-litre Bentley, with ex-Humphrey Cook engine, from Stanley Mann. 'I was never going to race this – it had the wrong engine, and I had a passion for a "Blower".'

As the company grew, so the possibility of acquiring such a car became realistic. 'I walked into Stanley Mann's one day, saw this "Blower" and asked him how much it would cost.' The car was immaculate but probably producing only about 130bhp, and it certainly did not handle. 'It was just awful.'

At the age of 45 Overington passed the ARDS test and took up racing with GP 8242. 'It was bloody useless!' The first event was the VSCC Pomeroy Trophy. It was raining, the track was greasy and the car slid round the corners at even 30mph. Overington puts his experience that day down to the fact that 'I can now drive the thing sideways. It was opposite-locking from the first event I ever did.' It is now generally

recognised that nobody today races a Bentley 4½-litre with quite the same verve.

The car has an original long-wheelbase chassis. It started life as a normally aspirated 4½-litre but was one of the first to be converted. This, thinks Overington, may be a good thing as far as he is concerned. Many of the original 50 production 'Blowers' are no longer correct to period, but 'mine probably behaves more in line with what a Birkin car did', he thinks.

The engine has been taken apart and fitted with larger carburettors, as Birkin would have done. The compression ratio was increased and it was ensured that the supercharger and brakes were working correctly. The car was transformed, with the engine now giving about 212bhp. From then on Overington raced it intensively, competing at such tracks as Pau, Spa, Angoulême, Magny Cours and Le Mans as well as the majority of UK circuits. 'The car got raced ragged. At the Le Mans Classic it broke the diff and the half-shaft. The supercharger also started playing up and had to be rebuilt. The compression ratio was also reduced and the power just surged out of it. It will now give the Talbots a run for their money and can beat BMW 328s down the Mulsanne Straight.'

Overington may be known for racing his 4½-litre hard – 'when I race, it is on its limit' – but it must be pointed out that he changes the oil every time he races it and is fastidious in its maintenance. He admits that, against the Talbot 105s, with their far superior brakes, his original-spec car is uncompetitive. Up against a Mercedes-Benz SSK at Goodwood and looking forward to a re-run of Le Mans 1930, Martin reckoned he could be competitive, always assuming that – as should have been the case with Caracciola – the driver did not keep the supercharger in play very often. He was told that these days, the supercharger on the SSK can be kept in almost indefinitely. Such is progress; the playing field in historic racing is far from level. 'The Bentley does well, though – at the Le Mans Classic it was about sixth on the grid – but it is never going to win races.'

Overington drove the car from Turin to London in one day – with no problem at all, although the fuel consumption was pretty excessive, but then when racing this can be as low as four or five miles to the gallon. He adds: 'There is a huge difference in power output between hot, sunny days and cold, foggy days because of the supercharger.'

Overington met five-times Le Mans winner Derek Bell through the Hôtel de France, the famed location at La Chartre near Le Mans that he now owns. 'I walked up to him one day as he was putting his luggage in the back of a Bentley and asked him if he fancied driving my Porsche 962. He first drove the Bentley from the hotel to the circuit, and he was a natural.' Although Bell has only raced the car at the Le Mans Classic in 2012, he has driven it at a number of other non-race events. Unfortunately, the car had fuel starvation problems at Le Mans, continuously running lean at maximum speed. Eventually the barrels split. Bell has since driven either Overington's car or Bentley's own Birkin 'Blower' at the Schloss Dyke and Ennstal Classics.

Overington sums up: 'If it was one of the 50 would I drive it as I do? Probably no. So, for people to see a "Blower" that is true to form being driven in this way, you would probably have to see this car. It is what it is.'

XR 7117 – Ewen Getley

Ewen Getley had what was surely an original dream for an otherwise arguably undesirable 4½-litre Bentley that he had bought from the USA.

'What I wanted to do was to recreate the original supercharged car. The Paget team originally took a standard, ex-Bernard Rubin

BELOW An original dream in the making. Ewen Getley has been working on recreating the original supercharged 4½-litre. *(Ian Wagstaff)*

4½-litre car, added a supercharger and ran the car for a season. At the end of the season all the supercharged cars were taken back to Welwyn and were made identical. Features were changed, as were some of the chassis. Many of the simple, original prototype features were lost. The original car – YU 3250 – still exists (the first Airfix plastic kit depicts it) but I have come across a number of glass plate pictures of it in its original form. I just really like it as this, it's really simple and elegant with none of the quick action bullshit.

'I decided that, as I had a suitable car, I could recreate the prototype. Mine had a horrible, non-original body on it and was a mishmash of various bits and pieces, but it was a genuine 4½-litre. I'm trying to get it back to that original concept, just for a bit of fun.'

Work started in early 2014. Many of the castings no longer exist, so Getley has been busy on pattern work. The car will be as the original first raced, and thus make use of SU, rather than Zenith, carburettors. Half a year into the task, Getley moved to his present premises on the Bicester Heritage site and for a while the project was on the back burner. However, at the time of writing Ewen was 'back on the case' and was expecting to be shortly on the road.

GN 9294 – Nick Mason

Pink Floyd drummer Nick Mason, himself a veteran of five Le Mans and the current President of the Guild of Motoring Writers,

is the custodian of what had been his father Bill's 1930 4½-litre. Mason Senior, a noted documentary film director and himself a member of the Guild, had acquired the car just after the Second World War, and by the early 1950s was racing it regularly. 'Going to Silverstone with the Bentley was part of my childhood,' Mason recalls. 'I sat in the back on the way there, wearing the crash helmet because it could be pretty blowy. If things had gone well – or badly – we would stop to have dinner at the Bell at Aston Clinton on the way home. It was, by far, the most sophisticated eating that I had ever done.

'The Bentley Drivers Club would have meetings where the morning was taken up by sprints with circuit racing in the afternoon. These were full grids of Bentleys only, with a couple of races to include other marques.' Nick also vividly recalls an annual challenge between the BDC and the police training college at Hendon.

The car was looked after by Wally Saunders, who had been a riding mechanic for the Bentley team and whose brother-in-law was famed Bentley mechanic Wally Hassan. Vanden Plas-bodied, it was not widely modified but featured a hydraulic conversion to the brakes and triple SU carburettors, as well as the fitting of cycle wings rather than the huge, swooping steel ones with running boards.

Use of the Bentley was certainly not just confined to racing and Bill was known for using it on some of his camera shoots. Nick remembers it being taken to Brittany for the summer holidays. 'It was in the days when they used a crane to get a car on to the ferry, adding to the holiday excitement.'

Although Nick is an experienced racing driver himself, 'when it came to vintage cars I went down the 1.5-litre Aston Martin route, so I found the Bentley to be so much bigger and heavier. It was a bit large for my taste but I absolutely get the thing about Bentleys. Once you are in top gear you don't have to change down unless you come across something monumental!'

Nick has never raced the car himself and it now tends to be used primarily 'for family days' and has been present at all his family weddings, christenings and major birthdays.

BELOW Bill Mason presses on in the 4½-litre now owned by his son, Nick. (Nick Mason collection)

CH 8280 – Gregor Fisken

Noted historic car dealer Gregor Fisken has his own, very original 1929 Bentley 4½-litre – a rare car, being one of only nine 9ft 9in short chassis cars built. This was made for loyal Bentley customer J. Ward-Cox with 'Bertie' Kensington Moir, who was shortly to become a dealer in partnership with Reggie Straker, acting as agent. Perhaps its best-known, albeit brief, owner, though, was racer Bill Pacey who acquired the car in 1932. It was fitted with a standard sports four-seater Vanden Plas body – which cost £195 – adapted to fit the short chassis. It was built to a semi-Le Mans specification with double Hartford friction shock absorbers and the close-ratio, seven-pitch 'D' gearbox.

Throughout the late 1930s and 1940s it was owned by Philip 'Porky' Lees, one of the founder members of the VSCC Northern Section. Another Bentley racing driver was Bill Thompson, who changed the registration to WT 43 when he was among the subsequent owners. He was the first person to actually race the car (although Lees used it for trials), and did so for many years. Another owner, Peter Brennan, latterly raced the car prior to selling it to Fisken.

'I grew up in the north-east of Scotland,' recalls Gregor. 'The main source of conversation between myself, father and grandfather was cars, and the biggest excitement of the month was the arrival of *Motor Sport* magazine. I used to go straight to the back and the adverts of the great dealers such as Scott Montcrieff, Dan Margulies, Frank Dale and Stepsons. Father's aspiration was to have a 4½-litre Bentley. I remembered when one arrived, a four-seat drop-head coupé with body by Knibbs and Parkin, and that's what we were taken to school in during the early 1970s. Other kids' fathers had Jaguars or Triumph Stags. Our dad had a 4½-litre Bentley, which was way cooler.

'What changed my life was a Bentley Drivers Club trip to celebrate one of the great Le Mans victories. We went all the way from Scotland to Le Mans in the back of the vintage Bentley. We were invited to do some laps on the circuit; I remember coming round Tertre Rouge with my mother shouting for my father to slow down and my brother and I shouting "Faster, faster!" I thought then and there that I wanted to race at Le Mans.'

Fisken was to compete there four times, which included 18th overall in 2004 in a Porsche GT3. A year later he was leading the LMP2 class until his Lola broke. It is now his ambition to race the Bentley in the Le Mans Classic.

Fisken owned his first 4½-litre in the 1980s, having been able to buy back his father's car. However, in 1991 when he started Fiskens he needed to raise some money and it 'had to go'. He first saw CH 8280 in the paddock at a BDC Silverstone, realising that it looked slightly different to other 'W.O.s'. 'It looked really sporty.' He got to know owner Brennan, eventually telling him that if he ever wanted to sell the car, he would buy it. This eventually

ABOVE CH 8280 on display at the 2016 Windsor Castle Concours of Elegance. *(Ian Wagstaff)*

BELOW Bill Pacey, an illustrious former owner of CH 8280, signed this 1932 photo of the car. *(Gregor Fisken collection)*

happened and the car was taken to R.C. Moss in Melchbourne, Bedford, and restored to its original blue colour scheme. Graham Moss was restoring one of the original rexine fabric machines, so the car was re-covered in the genuine rexine cloth in time to show it at the 2016 Windsor Castle Concours of Elegance. It had already been used by Gregor on the Mille Miglia and Flying Scotsman, finishing both 'without any problem'.

The car retains its original Vanden Plas body with wood ash frame. It had lost its fabric many years ago and had been skinned in aluminium. This was unpicked by Moss in 2014 and the car was then covered with the reproduction of the original rexine cloth. It was re-trimmed

at the same time with the correct Connolly hide, dyed as was done in the 1920s where the natural hide was taken and sprayed with a nitrous cellulose colour. As in period, sprung coil springs were put in a hessian bag and covered with horsehair-filled and fluted cotton, 'which gives an incredibly comfortable sprung seat'.

At the time of writing R.C. Moss had covered eight cars with rexine cloth, Graham pointing out that conservation work can be carried out as well as restoration. The first cars to be so treated appeared at Pebble Beach in 2015. To date, three have been 4½-litre Bentleys, two Vanden Plas tourers and one saloon with body made by Maythorn, a Biggleswade-based coachbuilder that ceased trading in the early 1930s.

RIGHT Gregor Fisken also owns this Bentley 4½-litre with saloon bodywork by Maythorn and Son of Biggleswade. *(Ian Wagstaff)*

The 'single-seater' – private owner

UU 5871, one of the first two Birkin Blower cars to be produced, and what became 'the single-seater', started life with an ugly Harrison body. Birkin drove it in its first race, the 1929 Brooklands Six Hours. A second, two-seater Vanden Plas body was fitted that year, this being transferred to UR 9155 when UU 5871 was converted into a single-seater with an originally blue, Reid Railton-designed body. This was initially of a 1½-seater form with fabric skin stretched over a spring-steel lattice framework. The radiator was exposed while the supercharger, dumb-irons and carburettors were partially cowled. Railton later designed a new aluminium body to replace the original, this being made by A.P. Compton & Co of Merton.

Experiments were carried out with a Powerplus supercharger, but these proved inconclusive and an Amherst Villiers unit was re-installed. After the Paget team had been broken up, Dorothy retained the car, repainted red, to be used at Brooklands in sprint events and the BARC 500-miles.

According to *Motor Sport* editor 'Bill' Boddy, Birkin's friend and workshop manager, Clive Gallop, was known to drive the single-seater on the open road. It was so docile that he was able to use a route from the Welwyn works to Brooklands that even embraced some London traffic. If, during one of these runs, a plug oiled, Gallop would stop on the hill past the KLG spark plug factory, 'put in a new plug and roll-start down the rest of the gradient'. On one occasion he was said to have done 120mph on the Barnet Bypass.

The car was purchased by Peter Robertson Rodger in 1939 and rebuilt with a very narrow, two-seater body. In the mid-1960s, 'Rusty' Russ-Turner acquired it from John Morley and refitted the single-seater body but with a replacement radiator cowl shaped by Caffyns. The two-seater body was transferred to a 'bitza', UT 44, which is now in Argentina. Russ-Turner suffered a heart attack when racing the car at Silverstone and it then passed into the hands of George Daniels. Fittingly, Birkin's grandson James Buxton recalls taking his son, significantly named Henry, to see and sit in it during Daniels' ownership.

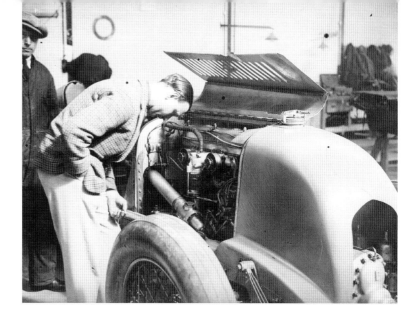

ABOVE 'Tim' Birkin closely examines the 'single-seater', which has recently been returned to its original specification by NDR. *(W.O. Bentley Memorial Foundation)*

In 2016 NDR Ltd finished restoring the single-seater, taking it back to its 1932 form. 'Racecars change from race to race and we decided to replicate its last race. Even then we had to make a compromise. Then it had three-inch downdraft SUs on the blower. Despite the fact that it was able to run on pump fuel because of the downdrafts (by wedging in venturis to reduce the choke size), they were actually done for methanol. Therefore we fitted the original, smaller side-draft carburettors.

'We removed the front brakes – in fact anything that should not be there. The cockpit was shortened back to its original size. We even found quite a few parts of the original bulkhead. When "Rusty" bought the car it was in a part-restored condition and his first idea was to put a two-seater body on it, so he fitted a standard 4½-litre bulkhead. When he decided to refit the single-seater body, as opposed to recommissioning the original fabricated aluminium and steel bulkhead, he cut down the 4½-litre, cast magnesium bulkhead and made it fit the single-seater body. Fortunately, George Daniels still had the mounting brackets and a couple of horseshoe frames. So often a car starts and finishes with a bulkhead. Its shape effectively dictates the shape of the radiator, the bonnet and the body behind. When Rusty owned the car it was always a bit misshapen in the middle because the bulkhead had compromised everything around it.

'We then restored the car mechanically from front to back. We discovered that the internals for the engine were all original, despite what had previously been thought.'

The single-seater was put up for auction

after the death of George Daniels. At the time there was a campaign to ensure that the car would never get export papers. Neil Davies looked carefully into this. To get a permanent export licence, cars over a certain age and value have to be assessed under the Arts Council's Waverley Criteria – is it so closely connected to the country's history and national life that its departure would be a misfortune, is it of outstanding aesthetic importance and is it of outstanding significance for the study of some particular branch of art, learning or history? An export licence can be refused, but after that someone has to be able to put up the money for the car within a set time to keep it in the UK.

According to Bonhams, a number of prominent and prospective customers were put off by the press coverage that had resulted, which probably worked out to Davies' customer's benefit, for he was able to buy it for £5.2 million, less than he had expected.

As soon as the car had been bought, export papers were applied for and the matter went before the Arts Council. Initially papers were refused, but this was appealed against. Matthew Collins QC –'a bit of a car buff' – then argued, using the Waverley Criteria, that the car should be allowed to leave the country, arguing that the nation already had some significant Brooklands Outer Circuit cars, such as the actual lap record holder Napier-Railton. Rather than demean the car, he said that we already had enough examples of its type. The car had to be taken to London and shown in Dean's Court behind Westminster Palace for the hearing. Initially, the application was refused on 'scientific grounds', because it had a dry sump, and that was quite new at the time. This meant that the nation had been given six months to come up with £5.2 million. Emotions raged, but such a sum could not be found and so, eventually, an export licence was granted. The new owner entrusted the car to NDR, from where after three years' restoration work it was moved to Germany, where it was, at the time of writing, in storage.

GF 3372 – Ron Warmington

It might be asked what a 5.3-litre car is doing here, but the car owned by Bentley Drivers Club Chairman Ron Warmington is an example of how an individual 4½-litre model can develop over the years. The car was originally registered as a Le Mans-bodied 4½-litre in 1929, the week after the Wall Street crash. Warmington now modestly describes it as 'a "Blower" replica'.

He had owned a Bentley Mk 6 Special for eight or nine years. 'I had enjoyed being a member of the BDC so much that I decided to take the plunge and go vintage.' Despite advice from his mechanic, the late John Guppy, that a 'Blower' would never run smoothly, that was what he desired, so, assisted by Stuart Fearnside, he set about searching for such a car. 'We really did look at some absolute rubbish,' he recalls. He eventually received a call from Stanley Mann saying that he had the car for him. This was GP 8242, the car that subsequently became Martin Overington's. However, Warmington had created a trust and one of the trustees thought it a bad investment, 'so he refused me permission, even though it was my money!'

Some time later there was another phone call, this time from Neil Davies, who thought he might have a client, John Lloyd, willing to sell a 'Blower'. However, Lloyd was on his way to Australia for three months and would be leaving the next day. Warmington had to get himself to Boars Hill just outside Oxford. Ron had taken the call on his way back from Cornwall, so he re-routed through Oxfordshire, having arranged for Fearnside to meet him there. Stuart already knew the car and advised purchase. That evening, Warmington and Lloyd shook hands on it for 'the best part of half a million pounds'.

The engine which had been expanded by Davies in 1990 to 5.3-litres by using 8-litre pistons and con rods, had been well used and, in Warmington's words, was 'clapped out', so every time he went on an event he was relegated to the back of the pack because of the amount of smoke that it was emitting. Thus Davies was called upon to rebuild the engine.

Further work on the engine has seen it fitted with such things as ceramic-coated pistons and large replica Birkin carburettors, 'which do "wonders" for the fuel consumption, as you might expect,' says Ron, with what might be described as a hint of sarcasm. 'After that, and once we had the mixture right, it has become

absolutely wonderful. I just can't fault the car. It has masses of torque. It also runs rather rich, but Neil wants it that way.' The car has also been upgraded to hydraulic brakes, 'which has a marvellous effect for racing'.

Much has been beefed up from the original, and that obviously carries a weight penalty. Warmington reckons that fuel consumption drops to about two miles per gallon when racing. 'You can smell the petrol going through it,' he says. 'Even on the road it only does about eight.'

The car has been a regular at the BDC MIRA and BRC Goodwood sprints, but in 2015 Warmington decided to go 'full-fledged racing'. VSCC meetings at Donington and Silverstone followed. 'I was always conscious of the possibility of trashing the car so I was never going to be a red mist racer.' The car also appears at other events, such as Flywheel at Bicester Airfield.

'I recall being overtaken on a French motorway by a Bugatti Veyron and, as we acknowledged each other, thinking that it was the supercar of today while mine was the supercar of 1929. It really is a head-turner.'

ABOVE BDC chairman Ron Warmington demonstrates his 5.3-litre 'Blower' during the 2016 Flywheel at Bicester. *(Ian Wagstaff)*

BELOW Ron Warmington's 'Blower' on a visit to Bentley Drivers Club headquarters at Wroxton, Banbury. *(Ian Wagstaff)*

BENJAFIELD'S RACING CLUB

Benjafield's Racing Club was formed in 1990, the concept of Stanley Mann – at the time one of the best-known exponents of the sporting merits of the vintage Bentley – and others. The club was named after Dr Dudley Benjafield, one of the best-known amateur 'gentleman' racers of vintage Bentleys in the 1920s, winner of the 1927 Le Mans and founder of the British Racing Drivers' Club. He was renowned for his promotion of the team good above his own interests, and he also ran an exclusive dining club for 'the Bentley Boys'.

The current Benjafield's Racing Club Chairman, Nigel Batchelor, says: 'Benjafield was noted for approaching his racing with the spirit of fair play and fierce but friendly competition: the club's ethos is to promote the competitive use of vintage Bentleys and other historic cars whilst preserving the spirit of Dr Benjafield and "the Bentley Boys".

'The club started to organise its own events that had not been done before: groups of vintage Bentleys drove on two occasions to Russia, led by its patron Prince Michael of Kent, and undertook trips to Denmark for the Copenhagen Grand Prix, rallies across India and the US and a memorable ten-countries-in-ten-days trip from London to Istanbul.

'During the winters there are dining-in nights and a major awards dinner where, as took place at the famous Savoy dinner in 1927, the vintage Bentleys join us at the dinner table. Everything is done in traditional style.'

Over the years that the club has been in

BELOW Members of the Benjafield's Racing Club, led by chairman Nigel Batchelor in his 1928 long-chassis 'Blower', arrive at Berkeley Square on their way back from Le Mans in 2016. Batchelor had shared his car with Katrina Kyvalova at the Le Mans Classic, making her the first lady to race a Bentley at La Sarthe. *(Actuarius)*

existence the membership has evolved, and after a slight lull in its activities in the early 2010s it has come back to the forefront of vintage and historic motor sport, again holding events that enable its members to experience things different to the current norm. In 2014 it organised the first 24-hour race for vintage cars for 75 years at Portimão in Portugal. In 2015 it restarted the club's annual sprint, changing the venue to Goodwood motor circuit. It also held a stubble-racing event in Norfolk, a very old form of motor sport where the crops are cut before racing takes place on the fields, creating dust and mayhem: it is thought this event was the first of its type in the UK for decades.

In 2016, in addition to the annual sprint, the club organised a group vintage Bentley entry to the Le Mans Classic where, true to the way it was done in the 1920s, the cars drove from the UK to the circuit, raced and then drove back to a champagne reception in Berkeley Square, the original haunt of the Bentley Boys of the pre-war era.

The club has a restricted membership, to ensure that it remains a manageable and homogeneous group, and prefers its members to have a vintage Bentley, or failing that a pre-war car of a type which would have been driven by Dr Benjafield and his friends. Of its present membership of 92, 74% are vintage Bentley owners. As a mark of the regard in which the club is currently held, it was voted Club of the Year at the International Historic Motoring Awards ceremony in November 2015.

For the future the club has plans to continue to provide premier events to showcase the vintage Bentley and other pre-war cars of its members and keep alive the spirit of 'the Bentley Boys era'. Included will be a Benjafield's 500, similar in concept to the Brooklands 500 which ran from 1929 to 1937 and which, as Batchelor points out, 'has never been held since'.

ABOVE Stubble racing – an excellent way of enjoying oneself in a Bentley 4½-litre…. *(Courtesy William Medcalf)*

BELOW …or of perhaps just getting lost. *(Courtesy William Medcalf)*

Chapter Six

Individual chassis histories

A total of 685 normally aspirated and supercharged Bentley 4½-litres were built. The vast majority never took to the racetrack. However, there were a handful – cars entered by the Bentley factory, Dorothy Paget and by a few private individuals – which, between 1927 and 1930, helped to create a legend by their exploits at Le Mans, Brooklands and in Ireland.

OPPOSITE 'I am simply a custodian.' – Dr Ian Andrews, Bentley 4½-litre owner. *(Ian Wagstaff)*

ABOVE UR 6571 in all its glory during Neil Corner's ownership.
(Neil Corner collection)

Amongst the 630 unblown and 55 blown Bentley 4½-litres built a number stand out as racing cars by virtue of having competed in the great endurance races during the 1920s and 1930s. As with many other racing cars, identities may have become blurred as rebuilds and even changes of registration plate have occurred. (William Medcalf points out the new car tax that was in play in the 1950s meant owners only paid £5 if they had a 'new' car. A lot of pre-war cars, including Bentleys, were consequently re-registered as being 'new' to take advantage of this tax regime. Such cars gained a new registration number and, in many cases, a new chassis number. Although it may be alarming to a reader today, the practice was not uncommon at that time.)

It should also be remembered that Bentley

did not build complete cars in-house. The works delivered the rolling chassis to the coachbuilder of the owner's choice for the necessary finishing as agreed between the owner and the coachbuilding firm. These firms varied in quality and ability. For any Bentley to receive its five-year guarantee, cars would need to be returned to the works and inspected to ensure that the designer's drawing of clearances and access points had not been compromised by the coachbuilder. Effectively, the coachwork was merely a dress that the car wore and could be exchanged at will as styles and functionality dictated. It was not uncommon for racecars to exchange bodies frequently to meet the regulations of different events. There were even owners of road-going cars who would change the body to mark the seasons.

The problem of identity is not a new one. Writing in a specialist Bentley Drivers Club publication four decades ago, the club's then president Stanley Sedgwick said: 'The motoring historian is on delicate ground indeed when trying to decide whether or not a particular car contains sufficient parts of the car which was delivered new over 40 years ago to merit continued identification with that original chassis.

'Many of the supercharged 4½-litre Bentleys still in existence still retain the same chassis frame and engine and quite a few the same body – as when they left the factory. At the opposite end of the spectrum there are some cars which have been made up from bits – some original, some manufactured – gathered together from a dozen sources or more.

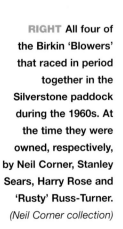

RIGHT All four of the Birkin 'Blowers' that raced in period together in the Silverstone paddock during the 1960s. At the time they were owned, respectively, by Neil Corner, Stanley Sears, Harry Rose and 'Rusty' Russ-Turner.
(Neil Corner collection)

Between these two extremes there are probably nearly as many shades of variation from the original as there are cars surviving.'

As Neil Davies asks, 'How much of the original car do you need? If you have the one remaining component and build a whole car round it, is it then the original car?'

Although the identity of no 4½-litre has reached the heights of controversy attained by the Bentley Speed Six 'Old Number One', which became the centre of a court battle in the 1990s, there is at least one case where one of them might now be said to have spawned two different cars. For some of the others, such as Bentley's own No 2 Paget Team Car or the privately owned unblown BRDC 500-mile winner, the provenance is such that there can be no doubt of their identity.

While Chapter Five highlights examples of the wide variety of competition 4½-litres still in existence, those that raced in the great endurance events of the late 1920s and early 1930s are listed as follows.

Chassis no	ST 3001	
Registration no	YH 3196	
The first production 4½-litre. 'Mother Gun'.		
1927	Le Mans	Crashed
	Grand Prix de Paris	1st
1928	Brooklands Six Hours	8th
	Le Mans	1st
1929	Le Mans	2nd
	Tourist Trophy	Flagged-off
	BRDC 500-miles	Retired

'Mother Gun' was first registered in 1927, its owner being Woolf Barnato. It was the only 4½-litre at Le Mans that year, where it was a victim of the 'White House' crash, but it

1928. Le Mans Winning Car landing at Dieppe before Race.

TOP The soon-to-be-victorious 'Mother Gun' landing at Dieppe on its way to Le Mans in 1928. *(W.O. Bentley Memorial Foundation)*

CENTRE 'Mother Gun' in the pits at Le Mans, 1928. *(W.O. Bentley Memorial Foundation)*

RIGHT 'Mother Gun's' original, RAC-stamped cylinder block at Vintage Bentley Heritage. *(Ian Wagstaff)*

ABOVE Richard Marker fitted a single-seater body to ST 3001, which duly became the Bentley Jackson Special. It is seen here ahead of three other cars in the 1934 BRDC 500-miles. Fourth is the larger Bentley-engined Barnato-Hassan Special on which Wally Hassan was working when he was asked to build the 4½-litre-engined Pacey-Hassan. *(W.O. Bentley Memorial Foundation)*

subsequently became the most successful of the 4½-litre cars, winning at Montlhéry a couple of months later and coming first again when it returned to Le Mans the following year. In 1929 it was again the first of the 4½-litres at La Sarthe, being beaten only by the lone Speed Six. The car was bought in 1932 by Richard Marker, who fitted a single-seater body two years later and then a 6½-litre engine. Over the winter of 1936/37 it was rebuilt by R.R. Jackson using a new frame and another single-seater body, after which it was known as the Bentley

Jackson Special. Due to the various changes made to this car, it eventually became possible for two cars to exist that both have parts that can be traced back to the original – a Bentley Jackson Special and a 'Mother Gun' now 'survive' as separate cars, one in Germany, the other in Japan, while the original RAC-stamped cylinder block is on display at William Medcalf's Vintage Bentley Heritage.

Chassis no		KM 3077
Registration no		YV 7263
1928	Brooklands Six Hours	3rd
	Le Mans	5th
	Nürburgring	8th
	Tourist Trophy	5th
	George Boillot Cup	5th
1929	Le Mans	Retired
	Brooklands Double Twelve	Retired
	Montlhéry single-handed 24-hour record attempt	
	Irish GP	4th
1931	Le Mans	Retired
	BRDC 500-miles	Flagged-off

The fifth-placed car at Le Mans in 1928, where it carried the number three, this was sold in the USA in the late 1950s. It was to race at Le Mans three times, once after the factory had withdrawn from racing, being the car that Bevan and Couper used for the 1931 24 Hours as well as the BRDC 500-miles. Its best result was its

BELOW After the factory had withdrawn from racing Bevan and Couper entered YV 7263 for the 1931 Le Mans 24 Hours. *(W.O. Bentley Memorial Foundation)*

first outing, when Birkin took it to third place on handicap while winning the Barnato Cup for the furthest overall distance.

Chassis no	KM 3088	
Registration no	YW 2557	
1928	Le Mans	Retired
1929	Brooklands Double Twelve	2nd
	Le Mans	3rd

This was one of the original Bentley Motors team cars that raced at Le Mans, where it retired in 1928 but was third a year later, the only car in the team left with a 'bobtail'. Actually the property of Sir Roland Gunter, it was sold to T.D.L. Rose in the 1930s. Although it was the only 'bobtail' team car to survive as such, replicas were subsequently made.

Chassis no	TX 3246	
Registration no	YW 5758	
See also pages 114–116.		
1928	Tourist Trophy	7th
1929	Le Mans	4th
	Brooklands Six Hours	3rd
	Irish GP	5th
	BRDC 500-miles	1st

YW 5758 is one of only two original-bodied team cars in existence to have won a major blue ribbon race. The first owner of YW 5758 was Humphrey Cook, who initially raced it at the Newtownards TT in 1928. (Although it

ABOVE This rather unusual shot of YW 2557 clearly shows the bobtail used at Le Mans in 1928. *(W.O. Bentley Memorial Foundation)*

BELOW YMW 5758, then owned by C.T. Atkins, in attendance at the marriage of W.O. Bentley's niece in 1956. The chauffeur is Basil Mountford. *(Courtesy Dr Ian Andrews)*

RIGHT YW 5758
stands out, even in the
courtyard of Windsor
Castle. *(Ian Wagstaff)*

tourer' was bought in 1937 by Johnnie Green for his brother-in-law Lawrie Dawson. Green remarked upon its twin filler caps, which, he felt, were unique. Dawson raced it at Donington Park and Crystal Palace and competed with it in VSCC trials before the Second World War. Geoffrey Tew, who owned it in the immediate post-war years, observed that its steering was exceptionally light, noticeably more so than another 4½-litre he had previously owned, despite the latter being a much lighter car.

Chassis no		FB 3301
Registration no		UL 4471
1929	Brooklands Double Twelve	Retired
	Brooklands Six Hours	Retired
	Irish GP	N/S

Built by the factory to Le Mans specification and sold to Nigel Holder, this car competed in just two Brooklands endurance races, suffering a back axle problem in one and engine failure in the other. Holder's co-drivers were Birkin and Rubin respectively. Among its subsequent pre-war owners was Marcus Chambers, a Le Mans class winner with an HRG and later the legendary competitions manager of BMC and then Rootes. Its next owner, John Lander, accompanied Chambers on his 1938 trip to Le Mans, as a result of which he was allowed to drive it on the track during a practice session for the 24-hour race.

Chassis no		HB 3402 (s/c)
Registration no		UU 5871

The first s/c 4½-litre, which became the single-seater track car. See also pages 123–124.

1929	Brooklands Six Hours	Retired
	Irish GP	3rd
	Tourist Trophy	11th
	BRDC 500-miles	Retired (last race before conversion to single-seater)
1930	BRDC 500-miles	9th
1931	BRDC 500-miles	Retired
1932	Brooklands lap record	137.96mph

competed as a factory team car it was, like the others at the time, privately owned.) In 1929 Frank Clement and Jack Barclay took it to victory in the BRDC 500-mile race at Brooklands. This was the fastest long race in the world at that time and the first British Racing Drivers' Club event to be held. It continued to race post-war in the hands of Harry Rose and his daughter Ann Shoosmith. Although no longer raced, its current owner, Dr Ian Andrews, both uses it and takes it to commemorative events here and abroad.

Chassis no		NX 3451
Registration no		UU 5580
1929	Brooklands Double Twelve	11th
	Brooklands Six Hours	8th
	Irish GP	7th
	BRDC 500-miles	5th

This initially green, Le Mans-specification car was bought by William 'Bummer' Scott in 1929. He raced it both with his wife Jill and with Jack Patterson. For the Irish GP, it was allied to the factory team. For its final race in Scott's ownership, the BRDC 500, it was driven by Tim Rose-Richards and Cecil Fiennes. It was sold in 1930 and, after passing through a couple of hands, the then 'black aluminium panelled

LEFT It was said that the single-seater was in a 'bad mood' when Birkin drove it in the 1930 BRDC 500-miles. Here Eyston and Hall line up against him in their more conventional 'Blowers'. *(W.O. Bentley Memorial Foundation)*

One of the first two Birkin 'Blower' cars to be produced, the 'No 1 Team Car' was originally fitted with a Harrison body, which was replaced later in the year by one from Vanden Plas. This was a special two-seater body made of spring steel hoops laid over aluminium longitudinals. It was later removed and transferred to UR 9155.

The famous single-seater body, first coloured blue and later red, was designed by Reid Railton and made and fitted by A.P. Compton & Co of Merton. A different supercharger, a Powerplus, is thought to have been fitted for one meeting in 1931, but, with no increase in performance, this was removed, the standard Amherst Villiers

BELOW Brooklands is a blur as Birkin blasts the single-seater around the great Weybridge bowl. *(W.O. Bentley Memorial Foundation)*

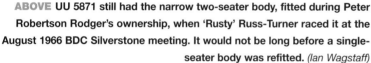

ABOVE UU 5871 still had the narrow two-seater body, fitted during Peter Robertson Rodger's ownership, when 'Rusty' Russ-Turner raced it at the August 1966 BDC Silverstone meeting. It would not be long before a single-seater body was refitted. *(Ian Wagstaff)*

ABOVE RIGHT Another shot from the Bentley Drivers Club 1966 meeting shows UU 5871's Brooklands-style exhaust system. *(Ian Wagstaff)*

BELOW Bentley Motors' own Birkin 'Blower' UU 5872 was used to convey (left to right) Guy Smith, Tom Kristensen and 'Dindo' Capello down the Champs-Élysées following their win in the 2003 Le Mans 24 Hours. The second-place drivers – left to right David Brabham, Johnny Herbert and Mark Blundell – had to make do with one of the 50 production 'Blowers'. Ahead of them was the winning Speed 8 driven by Derek Bell. The crowded conditions proved a problem. As Bell later exclaimed, 'The only time I blew up a Le Mans engine and it wasn't in the race!' *(Bentley Motors)*

supercharger then being modified. The car was the last of the 'Blower' Bentleys to be retained by Dorothy Paget, who kept it until 1939. It was then rebuilt with a narrow two-seater body, although it was reunited with its original single-seater body in the mid-1960s. It is now in private ownership in Germany.

Chassis no	HB 3403 (s/c)	
Registration no	UU 5872	
See also pages 113–114.		
1929	Irish GP	8th
	Tourist Trophy	Crashed
1930	Brooklands Double Twelve	Retired
	Le Mans	Retired
	Irish GP	4th
	Tourist Trophy	Crashed
	BRDC 500-miles	2nd

Perhaps the most famous of all the 4½-litre 'Blower' Bentleys, this is the 'No 2 Team Car' with which Birkin harried Caracciola in 1930. The car was originally built in 1929 on a 10ft 10in wheelbase frame and high-sided body. Badly damaged at Ards, it was rebuilt on a 9ft 9½in chassis with four-seater Vanden Plas body. In 1930 Birkin set the ultimate lap record for the 10.153-mile Le Mans circuit with it, the car finishing second in the Brooklands 500 later in the year, equalling the best result achieved by a 'Blower' Bentley. Amongst the various subsequent owners

ABOVE Being Bentley Motors' own, the No 2 Birkin Team Car is the natural subject for a press release photo. *(Bentley Motors)*

RIGHT Part of the original fabric of UU 5872 is still kept at Bentley Drivers Club headquarters in Wroxton, this piece still showing its racing number from the 1930 BRDC 500-miles. This sample was still on the car when Tony Townsend 'pulled it out of a barn' in the mid-1950s. Much of its life has been spent in an envelope, and it has therefore not suffered from the ravages of UVF. The fabric is occasional borrowed by R.C. Moss to ensure the accuracy of its reproduction of the rexine cloth, which has been used on such cars as Gregor Fisken's CH 8280, and to check on the original colour. Graham Moss points out that three different greens were used by Bentley Motors during its time in racing, the lighter Parsons Napier green that only appeared on the 3-litre models, 'International Green' as used on the 4½-litres, and so-called 'Le Mans Green', as seen on the Birkin 'Blowers' as well as the Speed Sixes. *(Ian Wagstaff)*

RIGHT At one stage, the Sears and Corner families both owned former Paget Team 'Blowers'. Jack Sears is seen here in the No. 2 Team Car talking to Neil Corner's wife, Freda. *(Neil Corner collection)*

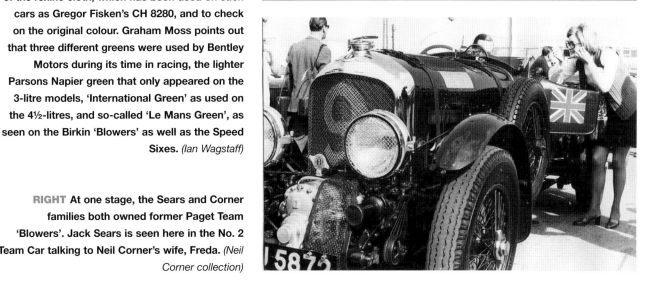

were M.N. Mavrogardato, Stanley Sears and his son Jack (the latter having it restored by Tony Townsend) and Victor Gauntlet. Now owned by Bentley Motors itself, it remains a superb and original example of a 'Blower'.

Chassis no		HB 3404/R (s/c)
Registration no		YU 3250
1929	Tourist Trophy	Retired
1930	Brooklands Double Twelve	Retired
	Le Mans	N/S
	Irish GP	65 laps
	Tourist Trophy	11th

The Paget 'No 3 Team Car', this started life as a standard 4½-litre supplied to Bernard Rubin. The first Amherst Villiers supercharger was fitted to this Vanden Plas-bodied, 10ft 10in-chassis car. After its career as a team car, it reappeared – re-registered as JH 3115 – for a couple of meetings at Brooklands, Charles Turner driving it to victory in the Addlestone Senior Short Handicap that Easter. The car also competed in the Southport 100-mile race and the Lewes speed trials. It was noteworthy post-war for having been raced by Harry Rose and his daughter Ann Shoosmith. It is now based in the USA.

Chassis no		HR 3976 (s/c)
Registration no		UR 6571
1930	Brooklands Double Twelve	Retired
	Le Mans	Retired
	Irish GP	64 laps
	Tourist Trophy	Flagged-off
	French GP, Pau	2nd (uncertain identity, ran in stripped-down form)
	BRDC 500-miles	Retired
1932	Le Mans	Crashed
1933	Le Mans	Crashed

The 'No 4 Team Car' performed arguably the most remarkable feat by a 'Blower' Bentley when it came second in the 1930 French Grand Prix, competing against a field of GP machinery. It was also the last such car to compete in the Le Mans 24 Hours, having been prepared by Birkin and Couper for Trévoux to enter in 1931 and 1932. Peter Robertson-Rodger later entered it for minor races at Brooklands and Donington. There has, in the past, been some confusion over the identities of this and UU 5872, caused when its UR 6571 registration plate was allocated to the No 2 Team Car in the mid-

BELOW UR 6571, seen here (No 5) in 1932, was the last 4½-litre 'Blower' to compete in the Le Mans 24 Hours. *(W.O. Bentley Memorial Foundation)*

1930s. Subsequent owners R.C. Murton-Neale and Peter Robertson-Rodger both raced it at Brooklands, in 1934 and 1936 respectively. At one stage the car was owned by noted historic racer Neil Corner. Harvey Hine recalls Corner asking him to drive it from Dieppe to Le Mans for a BDC event at La Sarthe circuit. 'It was a great handling car,' he says. It became part of the Ralph Lauren collection in 1988.

Chassis no	UR 9155 (s/c)
Registration no	HR 3977

The 'No 5 Team Car' had no racing history, although it is believed to have been built out of parts from Birkin and Couper's stores in 1931. It received the 1929 500-mile body from UU 5871 when this was reconstructed as the single-seater. It was sold to a shooting friend of Birkin, David Cuthbert. During the Second World War it was timed at 137mph on a stretch of Norfolk road unofficially closed for the occasion by the army. UR 9155 only really became a competition car after the war when subsequent owners, Grand Prix drivers Jack Fairman and Geoff Richardson respectively, entered it for VSCC races. It was further raced in the 1950s

ABOVE The No 4 Paget Team Car was, for some years, the property of leading historic racecar driver Neil Corner. *(Neil Corner collection)*

BELOW In 1968 UR 6571 won the Bentley Drivers Club Concours in Kensington Gardens and was invited to the Dorchester Hotel, London, for the club's annual Dinner Dance. *(Neil Corner collection)*

ABOVE **The No. 4 Team Car on display at Silverstone during Neil Corner's ownership.** *(Neil Corner collection)*

BELOW **As elsewhere, EXP5 YW 3774 was used as the 'spares car' at Newtownards in 1928. It is seen here with the Humphrey Cook-owned YW 5758. For that year's TT the cars were prepared and stored in a coach house at Kane's Yard near the town square. EXP5 was made from racing components and would be taken to events as a convenient way of transporting spares.** *(Dr Ian Andrews collection)*

by Alick Pitts, who became the first winner of the VSCC Seaman Memorial Trophy's vintage class with it. He later hill climbed and sprinted with it and was a regular competitor at the Brighton Speed Trials, where it became the first vintage car to record a sub-30-second time. It was acquired in 1999 by the late Bruce Spollon and is now owned by his son Guy.

Chassis no		FT 3209
Registration no		YW 8936
1930	Brooklands Double Twelve	Retired

Built to Le Mans specifications with Vanden Plas sports four-seater body, this 4½-litre was first owned by M.O. Durand and used extensively for competition in hill climbs and trials. Its only major race was the 1930 Brooklands Double Twelve, where it was driven by Durand and T.K. Williams.

Chassis no		DS 3556
Registration no		UV 3108
1930	Tourist Trophy	12th

This car was built to Le Mans specification with a Vanden Plas body for Eddie Hall. It was re-bodied in 1931 by Wylder. In addition to driving in the 1930 TT, finishing second in class, Hall competed with it regularly during the 1930s. He won the 1930 Mountain Handicap at the Brooklands Whitsun meeting and also had several sports car wins at the Shelsley Walsh hill climb.

Other Bentley 4½-litres to have competed pre-war included:

Chassis no	RL 3448
Registration no	AG 4106

This was raced at Brooklands by Frank Elgood in 1937–39, latterly using an engine bored out to 4,487cc. Successes included first in the 1937 October handicap and the 1938 Whitsun meeting (Locke King Trophy), the Baddeley Trophy in the 1938 MCC One Hour Trial, and third in the 1938 Dunlop Jubilee Race, when it is thought to have set the fastest lap by a road-going 4½-litre at Brooklands.

Chassis no	SL 3067
Registration no	YU 4453

This was originally bodied as a Gurney Nutting saloon but was re-bodied in the late 1930s and driven to fifth place at the 1936 BARC Brooklands October meeting.

Chassis no	MS 3930
Registration no	YY 3692

One of the 50 standard factory built 'Blowers', this was raced at Brooklands in 1934 in the Merrow Mountain Handicap at the BARC Whitsun meeting, driven by Esplen.

In addition, EXP5 (YW 3774) was built by the works to take to Le Mans in 1928, 1929 and 1930, incorporating spare parts for the team cars and being used as transport for the mechanics.

THE PACEY-HASSAN

A number of what started life as 3-litre cars now have 4½-litre engines. With the exception of the prototype 4½-litre ST 3001, which was built on what was basically a 10ft 10in 3-litre chassis, none of these have any significant history and are outside the remit of this book. However, there is one racing car that made use of an unblown 4½-litre power unit that it would be remiss not to include.

Wally Hassan and Wally Saunders, who had both been mechanics on the works team, built a single-seater Brooklands track car for Bill Pacey. The Pacey-Hassan was constructed in a garage in North Wembley in 1935, during which time Hassan was also working on another Brooklands racer, the larger-engined Barnato-Hassan Special. Use was made of basic Bentley mechanicals and a Hassan-designed frame that was built by Rubery Owen.

Pacey won first time out with the car at the 1936 Brooklands Easter meeting. For the rest of the year it was handicapped out of the results, while the 4½-litre engine broke during the BRDC 500-miles. For the following season a new engine was created using a 3-litre block on a Blower 4½-litre crankcase with Blower rods and crankshaft and a Zoller supercharger. The handicappers still had it in their sights, and after it had finished eighth in the 1937 BRDC 500-miles Pacey gave up trying. It was not to race again until after the Second World War. At one stage it was rebuilt into a road car but was eventually refitted with a single-seater body similar to the original and a 4½-litre engine.

Interestingly, the competition history of

Pacey and Hassan shows the mindset and struggle for supremacy in motor sport. In later years, Wally Hassan stated that when he built the Pacey he did so with extra compression plates under the cylinder block which reduced the car's performance. After each successful outing the handicappers would up the ante. In reply Wally Hassan would strip and 'check' the engine and on occasion 'forget' to replace all the compression plates. This increased the compression ratio, giving a better performance next time out, much to the bafflement of the handicappers. However, after a whole season's racing a finite resource of compression plates was exhausted and so the car could no longer be competitive and retired from racing. It was good while it lasted and the Pacey-Hassan once lapped the outer circuit at Brooklands at over 129mph.

BELOW The restored Pacey-Hassan was used as the pace car for the Benjafield's Racing Club 24-hour race at Portimão, also making an appearance, as seen here, at the club's Goodwood sprint in 2016. (*Actuarius*)

Epilogue

It certainly was not the best of the Cricklewood Bentleys. Indeed, in supercharged form W.O. positively disliked it, but for the man in the street the 4½-litre model is the archetypal Bentley. This has nothing to do with the technology of the car, nor with its racing results. As far as endurance races were concerned, other than the victory for an unblown 4½-litre at Le Mans in 1928 there were only the wins in the far lower-key 24-hour race at Montlhéry and the following year's Brooklands 500-miles, where one was classified in first place. In addition, there was the 1928 Brooklands Six Hours where one covered the furthest overall distance but only finished third on handicap.

The awe in which the 4½-litre cars are held has more to do with image and charisma. Otherwise, why was it that both Airfix and Scalextric chose them for their popular model ranges? Perhaps it is really down to two people, one a fictional character, the other a man whose life could, so easily, have come from a story book. The latter has to be 'Tim' Birkin, his polka-dot scarf flying in the breeze as he takes on the foreign hordes or blasts round Brooklands in the single-seater 4½-litre. He may not have actually won at Pau, but who else has ever taken on Grand Prix machinery with a road-going sports car to such effect?

As far as the Le Mans 24 Hours 4½-litre story is concerned, it is not the defeat of the Americans in 1928 that stands out but the glorious, doomed battle with the German (and remember, this is little more than a decade since the Great War) Mercedes-Benz two years later. Who, by comparison, remembers that it was actually a Speed Six Bentley that came first that year?

That Birkin versus Caracciola contest is said to have inspired the creator of the fictional character who has also become part of the Bentley 4½-litre legend. As explained earlier, Ian Fleming introduces us to James Bond's 'only personal hobby', a battleship-grey 'Blower', in *Casino Royale*. 'I put Bond in a Bentley simply because I like to use dashing, interesting things,' Fleming told *Playboy* magazine.

Despite the Le Mans win by the unblown 4½-litre, it is the blown version with its all-too-

visible supercharger protruding at the front that has become the stuff of legend. Dr Ian Andrews, the current owner of one of the most successful of all normally aspirated versions, YW 5758, reflects on this. 'Undoubtedly, the general public has a fascination for the blown 4½-litre Bentley. When Birkin introduced the supercharged Bentley it was particularly fast but not necessarily particularly reliable. Nonetheless, "Tim" was a charismatic individual who left an indelible image upon the hearts and minds of the British public. The adoring public looked at what he had done against Caracciola in the Mercedes at Le Mans and thought "this is just fantastic". Indeed, Birkin was not only racing

for Bentley, he was also racing for King and Country. Thus the "Blower" Bentley entered into the consciousness of the British public from that day onwards. I think it is a little sad, however, to acknowledge that W.O. felt that the unreliability of the blown 4½ was one of the reasons why Bentley Motors passed into receivership in the summer of 1931.'

Philip Strickland, a founding Benjafield's Racing Club member, reckons that, while the 3-litre is 'the purists' car', as far as the 4½-litre is concerned 'it's the quintessential Bulldog Drummond, Ian Fleming Bentley, because of the Blower.'

Concludes William Medcalf, 'It really does fly the flag for Britain.'

Specification (Le Mans race cars)

	4½-litre	4½-litre Supercharged
Length	14ft 4½in (438cm)	
Width	5ft 8½in (174cm)	
Height	5ft 3in (160cm)	
Body	Aluminium bonnet; wood frame, clad with thin alloy covered with colour impregnated leather or 'Weymann Fabric Body'	
Chassis	Steel, ladder frame	
Wheelbase	10ft 10in (330cm)	10ft 10in (330cm) or 9ft 9in (297cm)*
Track (front)	4ft 8in (142cm)	
Track (rear)	4ft 8in (142cm)	
Front suspension	Beam axle with Woodhead semi-elliptic leaf springs, friction disc dampers	
Rear suspension	Live axle with Berry semi-elliptic leaf springs, friction disc dampers	
Steering	Worm and wheel	
Brakes	Mechanically operated 15.75in (400mm) diameter steel drums at each wheel	
Wheels	Steel, spoked, 21in (53.3cm) diameter	
Wheel width	6in (12.7cm)	
Tyres	6.00 x 21	
Fuel capacity	30 gallons (25 for 'bobtail')	35 gallons
Kerb weight	3,600lb (1,625kg)	3,800lb (1,725kg)
Engine type	Inline four-cylinder, single overhead cam	
Supercharger		Amherst Villiers 'Roots' type
Capacity	4.398 litres	
Bore & stroke	100mm x 140mm	
Power	130bhp @ 3,500rpm	175bhp @ 3,500rpm 182bhp @ 3,900rpm
Gearbox	Bentley 'C', superseded by 'D' (4 forward, 1 reverse gears)	

* *Because of the increased weight of the supercharger, and all of this being forward of the front-wheel centreline, the supercharged car worked the front tyres harder than the un-supercharged version and therefore handled with more understeer and worse traction. To combat this, several of the Birkin racecars were rebuilt to the original 3-litre shorter chassis specification to move some of the extra weight back on to the rear wheels.*

Birkin and the 4½-litre 'Bentley Boys' 1927–30

Sir Henry Birkin

Despite the fact that Woolf Barnato and Bernard Rubin were the only drivers to win Le Mans with a 4½-litre model, of all the 'Bentley Boys' one surely stands out when it comes to the story of the 4½-litre: Sir Henry Birkin, known to his friends as 'Tim'. After his heroics with such a car at the 1928 Le Mans, he went on to become the instigator of the blown version that did so much for the brand's legend and, in coming second in the French Grand Prix, scored the most successful result ever for a sports car against GP machinery.

Michael Burn, who ghost-wrote Birkin's autobiography *Full Throttle*, said that Birkin could be very determined. He also recalled him as 'very extravagant, generous … and fond of women. He wasn't at all a respectable person;

he was anything but stuffy. He was very good company and marvellous for a young man to admire.'

Burn described Birkin as 'very lithe, larger

ABOVE Birkin (right) with Barnato won the 1929 Le Mans 24 Hours for Bentley, albeit in a Speed Six.
(Bentley Motors)

LEFT Birkin seems to be absorbed by something in the cockpit as Kensington Moir and Benjafield lead the 'Blowers' away at the 1930 Tourist Trophy.
(W.O. Bentley Memorial Foundation)

ABOVE Intensely
patriotic, Birkin was
forced to drive an
Alfa Romeo with Earl
Howe when Bentley
withdrew from Le
Mans. It is doubtful if
Mussolini's telegram
congratulating the pair
on winning the 1931
race 'for Italy' would
have gone down well
with the baronet. (LAT)

in build, but still like a ballet dancer'. He was
athletic, but still smoked a lot. His attitude to
racing can be gleaned from a contemporary
press quote following the 1930 race: 'Exciting,
yes, but really one must not exaggerate. Three
tyres burst during the time I was at the wheel,
but they all burst in the right way at the right
place. I always think if your time is to come it
will come just as surely on the top of a bus or
anywhere else as on the motorcar racing circuit.'

Birkin was single-minded. Indeed, his
grandson James Buxton, a vintage Bentley
owner himself, believes that he was 'selfish in
the way that he put his own interests above
those of his wife and children.' Buxton also
wonders how a man of his 'diminutive stature
could have raced cars of this size on what were
essentially gravel roads for hour after hour. His
stamina must have been extraordinary.'

Birkin first appeared as a racing driver at
Brooklands in 1921, driving a 2-litre DFP. (Woolf
Barnato made his debut at the track at the
same time.) He was to say that he did not race
between 1921 and 1927 for business reasons.
However, there is surely significance in the fact
that this gap in his racing career coincided with
the period of his marriage to Audrey Latham,

daughter of Sir Thomas Latham, a director of
Courtaulds. The pair wed in 1921 but divorced
seven years later, an unusual occurrence for
those days. In 1927 Birkin reappeared at
Brooklands sharing a 4½-litre Bentley with his
brother Archie in the Six Hours race. He had
earlier divided the driving of the DFP with his
friend Clive Gallop, another former RFC pilot
(and later to become works manager at Birkin's
Welwyn operation), and it may have been
through his influence that Birkin first became
involved with the marque.

All the Bentleys in the 1927 Brooklands Six
Hours, except that of the Birkins, had duralumin
valve rockers, which broke up; only the
brothers' version had steel rockers. Birkin was
to record his disgust that, following a fuel stop,
he was replaced in the car by one of the other
Bentley drivers whose car had already retired;
he omitted to say that it was the experienced
Frank Clement. Problems with all the gears
except third meant that the car was only placed
third. The following year Birkin came home first
on distance in the Six Hours, although he was
beaten on handicap.

Birkin received a Brooklands 120mph badge
(for lapping the banked track in excess of that

speed) in 1929. He also won a BRDC Gold Star for Track Racing the following year. The fame of the man with the spotted blue-and-white silk scarf must, though, be based on his two Le Mans wins and his remarkable performance in the Pau Grand Prix.

Birkin became responsible for the 'Blower' Bentleys, the 4½-litre supercharged cars having persuaded the Hon Dorothy Paget to provide the funding to develop the 242bhp machines, using the supercharger expertise of Amherst Villiers.

With the Rolls-Royce takeover of Bentley in 1931 the company's racing ceased, and Birkin was forced to go outside the UK for his next winning mount for Le Mans. It was obvious that he felt very keenly the criticism that he and Earl Howe were to receive that year for using an Alfa Romeo, but the pair had little choice if they wanted to win outright.

He led the first five laps of the 1933 Tripoli GP in a Maserati 8C/3000. For an Englishman to lead such a race was a rare event. At half-distance he was still running second to Tazio Nuvolari, but poor pit work put him back to third before the controversial finish. It was to be Birkin's last race. Why he died is open to conjecture. He burnt his arm on the exhaust pipe during one of the pit stops and the wound turned septic. It is also thought that the malaria from which he had suffered since the Great War was a contributing factor. Initially it proved impossible to diagnose the complaint, but eventually blood poisoning was diagnosed and so began a three-week fight for his life during which his former Bentley teammate Benjafield, a medical doctor, hardly left his side. Two blood transfusions were performed, but Birkin's temperature continued to range between 101° and 103°, and he passed away that June. Michael Burn recalled: 'It seemed even then odd that he should have died.'

He was, believes James Buxton, 'probably a very sad person towards the end of his life. The impression that I got from my mother and grandmother was that he had burned his way through a very large inheritance, his racing career had been chequered and the "Blowers" hadn't been the success that he had hoped. I think the end of his life was rather pathetic, which I find rather moving.'

Woolf Barnato

Immensely wealthy thanks to his father's time in the South African diamond fields, 'Babe' Barnato saved Bentley Motors from receivership in 1926. Although then chairman of the company, he did not expect favourable terms as a driver. He won Le Mans in each of the three consecutive years that he entered the race (driving a 4½-litre in 1928) and was an excellent all-round sportsman, raced horses and boats as well as cars, boxed, and kept wicket for Surrey County Cricket Club. Despite his overall importance to the Bentley story, Barnato only raced a 4½-litre on three occasions.

BELOW Barnato was indeed an all-round sportsman. In keeping wicket for Surrey he was said by *The Illustrated Sporting & Dramatic News* to have 'no nerves', as one would 'expect… in a racing motorist'. (W.O. Bentley Memorial Foundation)

The Illustrated SPORTING & DRAMATIC News

SATURDAY, JULY 7, 1928. No. 2660.—Vol. CXX. Registered for transmission in the United Kingdom.
PRICE ONE SHILLING. Postage Rate: United Kingdom, 2½d.; Canada 1½d. Elsewhere abroad, 3d.

THE MILLIONAIRE RACING MOTORIST KEEPS FOR SURREY.
CAPTAIN WOOLF BARNATO BEHIND THE STUMPS AT THE OVAL, WITH R. W. SKENE BATTING FOR OXFORD UNIVERSITY.

This being the first year he has taken the game really seriously, Captain Woolf Barnato, the millionaire racing motorist, has made quite remarkable progress as a wicket-keeper. Since January he has been working really hard, with Strudwick coaching him, and has played all the cricket he could. His reward was to be taken to Southampton to play in his first county game last week and, on the strength of his showing in that match, to be chosen for Surrey against Oxford University against Hampshire. Without being spectacular, Captain Barnato is very safe. He has no nerves (nor would one expect nerves in a racing motorist), and is, moreover, very quick to learn.

Dr Dudley Benjafield

A Harley Street surgeon who specialised in bacteriology, the bald 'Benjy' dramatically won Le Mans in 1927 driving a 3-litre. He raced 4½-litres during 1928, joining Birkin's 'Blower' team the following year, his best result in such a car being second in the 1930 BRDC 500-miles. Benjafield tirelessly tended Birkin during his fatal illness and continued to race until 1936 when he had a couple of outings in an ERA. He was instrumental in the founding of the British Racing Drivers' Club.

'Jack' Barclay

The charismatic Jack Barclay makes but one appearance in the Bentley 4½-litre tale but it was a winning one, the motor trader sharing the victorious car with Frank Clement in the 1929 BRDC 500-miles. Barclay had raced extensively at Brooklands during the 1920s, beating Barnato there in 1924 and becoming a partner in a motor business during this time. This was to become the world's largest Bentley and Rolls-Royce dealership. Having retired from racing at the behest of his mother after she had bailed him out of a hefty gambling debt, he returned just once, to win the inaugural 500-miles.

ABOVE 'Benjy' (left) and Eddie Hall were placed second in the 1930 BRDC 500-miles. *(W.O. Bentley Memorial Foundation)*

BELOW A rare victory, Clement (left) and Barclay after having won the 1929 BRDC 500-miles. *(Dr Ian Andrews collection)*

Leslie Callingham

An executive with Shell, 'Snitch' Callingham was in at the beginning, sharing the first 4½-litre to race at Le Mans with Clement in 1927. As such, he is perhaps best remembered as one of the drivers involved in the infamous White House crash. He was to make just one more appearance in such a car, finishing third with Cook two years later in the BARC Six Hours.

Jean Chassagne

Frenchman Chassagne twice raced unblown 4½-litre Bentleys at Le Mans, famously running from the pits with a heavy jack in 1928 to replace the collapsed wheel on the car that he shared with Birkin. In 1930 he became a regular member of Paget's supercharged team, leading to a total of five endurance races in the 4½-litre cars. He had been a riding mechanic before the Great War, such appearances including the first-ever French Grand Prix in a Darracq. He began driving himself in 1911, finishing third for Sunbeam in the French Grand Prix a year later. Following service as a pilot in the French Air Force, Chassagne returned to race in such events as the French GP and the Indianapolis 500, leading the former in 1921 prior to retiring and finishing second in the inaugural Italian GP. The pinnacle of his career was victory in the 1922 TT for Sunbeam.

Frank Clement

Clement was the professional amongst the Bentley Boys. Initially a motorcycle racer, he joined Vauxhall and then Straker-Squire as a test driver, racing one of the latter's cars in the 1914 Tourist Trophy. Following war service in the Royal Engineers, he joined Bentley in 1920 as works manager and then manager of the Experimental Department. At Brooklands in May 1921 he became the first person to race a Bentley, following this shortly after by being the first to win for the marque. There followed more firsts – first to win Le Mans for Bentley, first to race a 4½-litre car there and, at Montlhéry, the first to win with such a car. He was also classified first in the 1929 Brooklands 500-miles, again with a 4½-litre. His track career ended when Bentley withdrew from racing.

Humphrey Cook

The wealthy Cook is perhaps best remembered as financing the start of ERA, Britain's most successful racing car manufacturer of the 1930s. However, he owned or was financially associated with three Bentleys that are accepted as factory team cars (none of the 4½-litres were actually owned by Bentley Motors), and raced his own 4½-litre a number of times in 1928 and 1929, with a best result of third in the BARC Six Hours with Callingham. It was Cook's own car that won the 1929 Brooklands 500-miles driven by Clement and Barclay. Earlier in his career Cook had raced a TT Vauxhall which, at one point was, like the 'Blower' Bentleys, supercharged by Amherst Villiers.

S.C.H. Davis

Sports editor for The Autocar and a semi-professional driver, 'Sammy' Davis worked with W.O. on his aero engines during the Great War. After the conflict he appeared as both driver and riding mechanic, acting as such in the 1924 and 1925 French Grands Prix. He first raced a Bentley at Le Mans in 1926, but, conscious of his privileged position at the magazine, accepted drives from a number of other British manufacturers. He shared the winning car with Benjafield at Le Mans in 1927, his first-hand

ABOVE The imperturbable Jean Chassagne in Ireland. *(W.O. Bentley Memorial Foundation)*

written account of the triumph adding to its lustre. His other notable success was winning the 1930 BRDC 500-miles in an Austin Ulster. Davis raced a 4½-litre Bentley just once, being classified second in the Brooklands Double Twelve the same year. He was the last surviving Bentley Boy.

Baron André d'Erlanger

An international banker, the sardonic and imperturbable d'Erlanger competed in just two endurance event with a 4½-litre Bentley, the 1929 Le Mans and the 1930 Brooklands Double Twelve, on both occasions co-driving with Benjafield. During the former race he hit another car reversing out of the Mulsanne sand bank but, reported *Motor Sport*, 'he forged on with a badly cut face and maintained a very creditable speed until the finish, despite these handicaps'. It was suggested by A.F. Rivers Fletcher that he did not become famous until he drove for the Bentley team. However, he had already raced a blown 2.3-litre Bugatti at Brooklands. His brother Gerard was a founder and commodore of the Air Transport Auxiliary during World War Two.

George Duller

A champion jockey, Duller began car racing in 1921. His was particularly active in the mid-1920s, winning at Brooklands and setting the World 12-Hours record with John Parry-Thomas. He won the Grand Prix de l'Overture at Montlhéry in 1925 for Talbot, making his Le Mans debut that year when he shared a Sunbeam with Henry Segrave. He was recruited by Barnato in 1926 to drive his Bugatti. His main contribution to the 4½-litre story was to share the winning drive with Clement in the Montlhéry 24 Hours. Drives after 1927 were rare but in 1930 he raced a 4½-litre for a second time, sharing a blown car with Birkin at the BRDC 500-miles.

Jack Dunfee

One of three brothers, all of whom raced, Jack Dunfee made three appearances in a 4½-litre Bentley, finishing just the once when he came second at Le Mans in 1929 with Glen Kidston. He began racing at Brooklands in 1925, subsequently owning a GP Ballot and Sunbeam as well as an Indianapolis Sunbeam. He was offered a drive in Birkin's 'Blower' team but took over the drive in 'Old Mother Gun'

BELOW Harcourt-Wood and Jack Dunfee were entered for the 1930 Le Mans 24 Hours by the Paget team. However, the car non-started, the official story being that it was being saved for the Spa 24 Hours. *(W.O. Bentley Memorial Foundation)*

when the supercharged cars were not ready. He subsequently drove for both the factory and Paget teams, sharing the winning 6½-litre 'Old Number One' in the 1929 Brooklands Six Hours with Barnato. Two years later, he and Cyril Paul won the BRDC 500-miles in the same car. He again shared 'Old Number One' in the 1932 500-mile race, this time with his brother Clive. The younger Dunfee was killed when the car went over the Members' Banking, and Jack then retired from racing.

M.O. de B. Durand

Durand shared his privately entered, unsupercharged 4½-litre with T.K. Williams in the 1930 Double Twelve at Brooklands. The car caught fire just after passing the paddock a couple of hours into the first heat. It continued, but later retired with back axle troubles. He also competed with the car in short handicap events at Brooklands, winning the Devon Long Handicap at the 1930 BARC Whitsun meeting.

George Eyston

Future Land Speed Record holder George Eyston appears just once in the 4½-litre story, sharing a 'Blower' with Harcourt-Wood in the 1930 BRDC 500-miles. Awarded the MC

for bravery in World War One, he raced first motorcycles and then cars, driving an Aston Martin in the 1926 RAC GP. He won that year's Boulogne GP in a Bugatti Type 39A and also shared a Maserati with Birkin in the 1931 French GP. His best result in the latter race came a year later, with third in an Alfa Romeo 8C. A serial winner at Brooklands, he turned to record-breaking in 1935, thrice taking the outright Land Speed Record in his self-penned *Thunderbolt*.

Jack Field

Jack Field is perhaps best remembered racing a former Malcolm Campbell Bugatti and an ex-record-breaking Sunbeam. He appeared just once in a major race in a 4½-litre, sharing with Jack Dunfee at the 1929 Brooklands 500.

Cecil Fiennes

Otherwise known as 'Turkey', Captain Fiennes competed in just one endurance race with a 4½-litre, the 1929 BRDC 500-miles. (He also raced Bentleys in shorter races at Brooklands, winning a handicap event there in 1923 with a bright yellow and blue car and later racing a 4½-litre in handicaps there.) It was said that he and Tim Rose-Richards did well to finish fifth

ABOVE The leaders are already away as the Durand/Williams 4½-litre (No 10) heads the rest of the massive field for the 1930 Brooklands Double Twelve. It was later to catch fire before retiring with a broken rear axle. *(W.O. Bentley Memorial Foundation)*

ABOVE The rain began to fall in the early hours of the afternoon during the 1930 TT. Eddie Hall (No 4) splashes on, driver and riding mechanic having swapped the linen helmets they wore at the start for 'hard hats'. *(W.O. Bentley Memorial Foundation)*

in the 500, averaging just under 99mph for the whole race. William Scott explained the Bentley was his second-string entry (he shared a GP Delage with Brian Lewis in his other car), and that both drivers were 'rather unknown at that time and were just close personal friends of mine … I told them both to take it easy in the race and finish – that was all, just as a second line of attack.'

Sir Roland Gunter

Gunter owned five Bentleys during the W.O. period including the 'bobtail' Le Mans 4½-litre YW 2557. Bentley mechanic Wally Hassan remembered calling on him at his house in Wetherby, Yorkshire, to examine one of his Bentleys for some defect or other. 'He was engaged in the car sales and service business in Leeds – quite a large establishment, I believe. I forget the name, but it might have been the Leeds Motor Co. He may have owned it, but certainly must have been a large shareholder. He was quite a good driver and kept up with the others at times.' Gunter was a close friend of Benjafield, with whom he raced a Lagonda and Alvis, the pair driving a 4½-litre version of the former in the 1935 Le Mans 24 Hours.

Eddie Hall

Hall raced and hill climbed during the 1920s, dominating the sports and touring class at Shelsley Walsh for a number of years, and also competing as a member of the British Olympic bobsleigh team in 1928. He purchased a Le Mans replica 4½-litre, which was used for

Brooklands handicap races and for the 1930 TT. Birkin then invited him to join the 'Blower' team for the BRDC 500-miles in which he finished second, partnered by Benjafield. His main success was victory in the 1933 BRDC 500-miles driving an MG K3. However, it was at Le Mans in 1950 that his stamina was underlined when he single-handedly drove his later, 3½-litre Bentley to eighth at Le Mans.

Beris Harcourt-Wood

Harcourt-Wood regularly drove for Birkin in 1929 and 1930, having previously had limited experience racing small Salmsons and Amilcars. W.B. Scott related how he and Harcourt-Wood were returning from Brooklands in two 4½-litres after a day's racing. 'We were both doing over a ton on that famous switchback where Kaye Don and Jack Barclay used to do far more, between Brooklands and Cobham.' As they swept past a large house a dog-collared clergyman on a bicycle 'swooped into the road in a wide curve. Beris did the only thing possible and went right on to the grass on the right side of the road. I could only take Beris *and* the clergyman on the inside of both of them. For a moment, the man of God was in the slipstream of two Bentleys 'doing a ton'. Scott observed that he was 'whirling like a dervish in the vortex of their passing [but] he was a good man; he didn't come off!' 'Some of us like Beris … were very young in those days and a bit wild,' wrote Scott. 'Don't get me wrong; we were very serious *in* a race and tried our hardest.'

E. Hayes

The inexperienced 'Frothblower' Hayes is another who raced in just one major contest with a 4½-litre, driving the then Richard Norton-owned 1928 Le Mans-winning car 'Old Mother Gun' in the 1929 Ards Tourist Trophy, in which he failed to finish.

Nigel Holder

Nigel Holder was a Bentley 4½-litre owner who raced his own car – built by the factory to Le Mans specification – in two of the major Brooklands races in 1929, sharing the drive with Birkin on one of these occasions. His uncle, Norman, had raced at Brooklands in 1913, competing in the meeting where W.O. had scored his first win with a DFP. Prior to the Double Twelve, Holder had little racing experience but was a director of Kensington Moir & Straker, described by author David Venables as 'an extramural motor-dealing activity of Bertie Kensington Moir'. Before the race, the latter took him to the Home Banking to show him how the faster drivers took the artificial corner there. When 'Sammy' Davis clouted the sandbank, he remarked that he would 'have to try and find an easier way'. Holder helped to build the prototype 'Blower' 4½-litre at Welwyn, following its first test run, which took place on the Barnet Bypass with his own car and accompanied by some of the mechanics.

Earl (Francis) Howe

Francis Curzon is another with just one appearance in the story, in this case the 1929 Le Mans when he shared a 4½-litre with Rubin. The fifth Earl Howe was to become influential in British motor sport – he was a long-time president of the British Racing Drivers' Club – but he did not start racing seriously until the age of 44. He shared the winning Alfa Romeo 8C-2300 at Le Mans with Birkin in 1931, the Bentleys now having left the scene. Unusually for an Englishman, he raced often on the Continent during the 1930s. A successful competitor in *voiturette* racing, first with Delages and then with an ERA, he made his GP debut at Monaco in 1931 in a Bugatti, finishing fourth there the next year.

ABOVE Earl Howe made just one appearance in a 4½-litre Bentley, sharing a car with Bernard Rubin at the 1929 Le Mans. *(W.O. Bentley Memorial Foundation)*

BELOW Howe went on to share the winning Alfa Romeo at Le Mans in 1931 with 'Tim' Birkin, subsequently writing the foreword for his friend's autobiography *Full Throttle*.

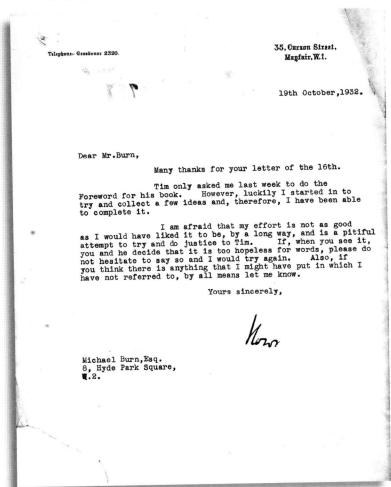

Glen Kidston

Kidston had experienced an adventurous time in the Royal Navy that included being torpedoed when on the aged cruiser HMS *Hogue* early in the Great War and later being trapped on the seabed in a submarine. He remained in the service after the war, rising to the rank of Lieutenant Commander. In addition to cars, he also raced motorcycles and speedboats. Having survived two aircraft accidents, his hitherto charmed life came to an end in 1931 when his DH Puss Moth crashed in Natal. Kidston's contribution to the 4½-litre story mirrors Jack Dunfee's, the pair sharing a factory and then a Paget car at Le Mans in 1929 and in the 1930 Double Twelve. With a substantial inheritance, thanks to his family's interests in the banking industry, Kidston was able to go racing and was one of the first to buy a Bugatti Type 35, scoring wins with the car at Brooklands. Friendship with Barnato brought him into the Bentley team and in 1930 they shared the winning drive at Le Mans.

'Bertie' Kensington Moir

Herbert Kensington Moir was one of those who lied about his age in order to join up during the Great War, the result being that he first joined the Royal Naval Air Service and then a team of 40 Austin armoured cars that fought in the Middle East. On returning from the war he joined Straker-Squire, going on to race one of its cars during the first three years of the 1920s. Work took him to Zenith Carburettors, while he became one of the first to race an Aston Martin in such events as the Isle of Man TT and the Brooklands 200-miles. He become service manager at Bentleys in 1922, later moving up to take charge of the Experimental Department. In his capacity as team manager for the company he became a well-known figure at the leading endurance events. He also raced the company's products in the early days, for example setting fastest time of the day at the Caerphilly hill climb in 1923, being part of the team at the Boulogne Speed Week and also competing at Le Mans in 1925. The bulky 'KM' did not race again until 1930, when Birkin persuaded him to replace Harcourt-Wood who, due to a tonsil problem, was unable to race one of the 'Blower' cars at Ards. Bentley himself was to recall that 'we did thousands of miles together testing the old Bentleys both abroad and in this country and [Kensington Moir] was one of the few drivers

with whom I felt entirely relaxed when being driven fast … He was also a racing driver of the highest class and much more would have been heard of him if circumstances had allowed him to continue to take part in racing.'

Jack Patterson

Jack Patterson was 'Bummer' Scott's partner for the 1929 Brooklands Six Hours, the pair finishing eighth on handicap.

Giulio Ramponi

Ramponi's early experiences of motor racing came as riding mechanic for Alfa Romeo greats Giuseppe Campari and Antonio Ascari. When riding mechanics were banned in Grands Prix for 1925 he remained in the racing department, as well as taking on the role of chief test driver for the Alfa Romeo 6C. He became a racing driver in his own right, success coming mainly in the UK where he won the 1928 Brooklands Six Hours. The following year he also came first in the Brooklands Double Twelve for Alfa Romeo, beating the Bentley 4½-litre of Davis and Gunter. His sole appearance in such a car came in 1930 when he was invited to drive one of the Paget 'Blower' versions at Le Mans.

As an engineer, he also worked with Whitney Straight and Dick Seaman, famously rebuilding a ten-year-old Delage for the latter to dominate *voiturette* racing. At one point Ramponi was in partnership with former Bentley mechanic Billy Rockell running the Alfa Romeo agency in Lancaster Gate, London.

Tim Rose-Richards

Welshman Tim Rose-Richards had just the one race in a 4½-litre (see Cecil Fiennes entry on pages 151–152). As observed above, both drivers were unknown at the time but, as 'Bummer' Scott wrote, 'Later on, of course, they both became quite famous in their own right.' Although never in a Bentley, Rose-Richards competed on six occasions at Le Mans including partnering past and future winners Earl Howe and John Hindmarsh and finishing third during three consecutive years. Drives in ERAs included partnering Raymond Mays in the 1935 International Trophy at Brooklands. He was killed in a flying accident in 1940.

Bernard Rubin

A close friend of Barnato, Australian-born Rubin was another wealthy man, his father having

ABOVE **Hands on hips, 'Bertie' Kensington Moir looks down on the Benjafield/ Ramponi 'Blower' at Le Mans in 1930.** *(W.O. Bentley Memorial Foundation)*

been a pearl dealer. He went on to become a property speculator. Despite no prior experience, he was paired with Birkin to drive a 4½-litre in the 1928 Brooklands Six Hours, the pair finishing second on the road but only sixth on handicap. A month later he helped Barnato to nurse 'Old Mother Gun' home to victory at Le Mans. He did not race again until the following year's Le Mans, when he again drove a 4½-litre. He joined the Paget team to drive a blown car in the two Irish races that year, crashing in the second of these and virtually bringing an end to a short racing career in which he had shown himself more than capable. He did, though, try and persuade Scott to enter his 4½-litre for Le Mans in 1931 with himself as co-driver, but Scott was already engaged to drive his Delage in the French GP a few days later and wanted the Bentley as his 'hack car'. It seems likely that Rubin's money helped to keep Birkin racing in 1931 and 1932. He was only 39 when he died of tuberculosis.

BELOW W O Bentley with the BRDC 500-miles winner towards the end of his life. (Dr Ian Andrews collection)

Jill Scott

Jill was the first wife of William Scott, with whom she shared a Bentley 4½-litre in just one major endurance race. She owned a Bugatti in her own right. She has been described as 'one of the great women drivers of her day and was the first woman to win a Brooklands Gold Star for a lap of over 120mph'. The pair lived in Old Byfleet to be near Brooklands. Jack Dunfee recounted a story about asking a policeman directions to their house and being advised not to go there. 'The Scots live there and they're all as mad as March 'ares. I saw one of them trying to jump off the roof with a parachute only the other day.'

William Scott

'Bummer' Scott, as he was known – a nickname he inherited from his rugby international uncle – had his own Bentley 4½-litre, UU 5580, which in addition to racing himself he entered for such drivers as Fiennes, Rose-Richards and Patterson. He also drove the car on one occasion with his wife Jill. Described as an 'all-round athlete' (he won a rugby blue at Cambridge and scored in the Varsity match), Scott was nearly always the fastest *into* a car when it came to Le Mans-style starts. Scott raced a variety of cars including a 1924 Grand Prix Sunbeam, 1927 GP Delage and various Bugattis and Amilcars, and had his own shed at Brooklands from where he bought and sold cars. In 1931 he entered the Delage for the French GP at Montlhéry, taking his 4½-litre Bentley with him as part of his équipe. 'We always had a very great and genuine respect for people like Tim Birkin and Sammy Davis,' said Scott. 'They were the "Prefects", we were the "Lower Fourth" in all our talk between ourselves. They were after all 15–18 years older than we were.'

T.K. Williams

Williams acted as Sir Roland Gunther's mechanic in the 1929 Double Twelve, returning for the same event the following year as co-driver for Durand. As such he had replaced Harcourt-Wood, who was suffering from severe tonsillitis.

Appendix 3

Long-distance race results 1927–34

1927
Le Mans 24 Hours:
Frank Clement/Leslie Callingham – DNF.

Montlhéry 24 Hours Grand Prix de Paris:
Frank Clement/George Duller – 1st.

Brooklands JCC/SMC 150-mile race (handicap):
Woolf Barnato – 3rd.

1928
Brooklands Essex Six Hours (Barnato Cup overall distance):
Sir Henry Birkin – 1st.
(**Essex Cup handicap** – 3rd.)

Bernard Rubin/Dudley Benjafield – 2nd.
(**Essex Cup handicap** – 6th.)
Frank Clement/Woolf Barnato – 3rd.
(**Essex Cup handicap** – 8th.)
Le Mans 24 Hours:
Woolf Barnato/Bernard Rubin – 1st.
Sir Henry Birkin/Jean Chassagne – 5th.
Dudley Benjafield/Frank Clement – DNF.
Nürburgring German Grand Prix:
Sir Henry Birkin – 8th.
Ards Tourist Trophy (handicap):
Sir Henry Birkin – 5th.
Humphrey Cook – 7th.
Boulogne George Boillot Cup (handicap):
Sir Henry Birkin – 5th.

BELOW Lull before the storm: the original racing 4½-litre, with its two 3-litre compatriots, heads the line-up for the 1927 Le Mans 24 Hours. *(W O Bentley Memorial Foundation)*

1929

Brooklands Double Twelve (handicap):
S.C.H. Davis/Sir Roland Gunter – 2nd.
William Scott/Jill Scott – 11th.
Frank Clement/Humphrey Cook – DNF.
Nigel Holder/Sir Henry Birkin – DNF.

Le Mans 24 Hours:
Glen Kidston/Jack Dunfee – 2nd.
Dudley Benjafield/Baron André
d'Erlanger – 3rd.
Frank Clement/Jean Chassagne – 4th.
Earl (Francis) Howe/Bernard Rubin – DNF.

Brooklands BARC Six-Hour race (handicap):
Humphrey Cook/Leslie Callingham – 3rd.
William Scott/Jack Patterson – 8th.
Sir Henry Birkin (s/c) – DNF.
Nigel Holder – DNF.

Phoenix Park Irish Grand Prix (handicap):
Sir Henry Birkin (s/c) – 3rd.
Beris Harcourt-Wood – 4th.
Humphrey Cook – 5th.
William Scott – 7th.
Bernard Rubin (s/c) – 8th.

Ards Tourist Trophy (handicap):
Sir Henry Birkin (s/c) – 11th.
Bernard Rubin (s/c) – DNF.
Beris Harcourt-Wood (s/c) – DNF.
E. Hayes – DNF.

Brooklands 500-miles (handicap):
Frank Clement/Jack Barclay – 1st.
Tim Rose-Richards/Cecil Fiennes – 5th.
Jack Dunfee/Jack Field – DNF.
Sir Henry Birkin/Beris Harcourt-Wood
(s/c) – DNF.

1930

Brooklands JCC Double Twelve (handicap):
Sir Henry Birkin/Jean Chassagne (s/c) – DNF.
Glen Kidston/Jack Dunfee (s/c) – DNF.
Dudley Benjafield/Baron André d'Erlanger
(s/c) – DNF.
M.O. Durand/T.K. Williams – DNF.

Le Mans 24 Hours:
Sir Henry Birkin/Jean Chassagne (s/c) – DNF.
Dudley Benjafield/Giulio Ramponi (s/c) – DNF.

Phoenix Park Irish Grand Prix:
Sir Henry Birkin (s/c) – 4th.
Beris Harcourt-Wood (s/c) – N/C.
Jean Chassagne (s/c) – N/C.

Ards Tourist Trophy (handicap):
Bertie Kensington Moir (s/c) – 11th.
Eddie Hall – 12th.
Dudley Benjafield (s/c) – DNF.
Sir Henry Birkin (s/c) – DNF.

Pau Grand Prix:
Sir Henry Birkin (s/c) – 2nd.

BRDC 500-miles Brooklands (handicap):
Dudley Benjafield/Eddie Hall (s/c) – 2nd.
Sir Henry Birkin/George Duller (s/c) – 9th.
George Eyston/Beris Harcourt-Wood (s/c) – DNF.

1931

Le Mans 24 Hours:
Anthony Bevan/Mike Couper (s/c) – DNF.

BRDC 500-miles Brooklands (handicap):
Antony Bevan/Mike Couper (s/c) – N/C.
Dudley Benjafield (s/c) – DNF.

1932

Le Mans 24 Hours:
Jean Trévoux/Pierre Brousselet – DNF.

1933

Le Mans 24 Hours:
Jean Trévoux/Louis Gas – DNF.

1934

Brooklands BARC 500-miles (handicap):
Richard Marker/Anthony Bevan – DNF.

BELOW The Bentley team of one 4½-litre (nearest camera) and two 3-litres being prepared prior to the 1927 Le Mans. *(W O Bentley Memorial Foundation)*

Appendix 4

Useful contacts

Bentley Drivers Club
(and W.O. Bentley Memorial Foundation)
W.O. Bentley Memorial Building
Ironstone Lane, Wroxton
Banbury
Oxfordshire OX15 6ED
Tel 01295 738 886
Website www.bdcl.org / www.wobmf.co.uk

Bentley Motors Ltd
Pyms Lane, Crewe
Cheshire CW1 3PL
Tel 01625 824844
Website www.bentleymotors.com

Bespoke Rallies
No 4 Telford Court
Littlemead, Cranleigh
Surrey GU6 8ND
Tel 01483 271 699
Website www.bespokerallies.com

Endurance Rally Association
St Mary's Road
East Hendred
Wantage
Oxfordshire OX12 8LF
Tel 01235 831221
Website www.endurorally.com

Brooklands Museum
Brooklands Road
Weybridge
Surrey KT13 0QN
Tel 01932 857381
Website www.brooklandsmuseum.com

Fiskens
14 Queens Gate Place Mews
Kensington
London SW7 5BQ
Tel 020 7584 3503
Website www.fiskens.com

BELOW Having earlier raced in the 2016 Le Mans Classic, Jurgen Ernst backs his 'Blower' into place outside Jack Barclay's showroom in Berkeley Square, London. *(Actuarius)*

ABOVE A Bentley
4½-litre on Historic
Competition Service's
stand at the 2016
Interclassics show in
Brussels.
(Wim Van Roy)

Hagerty Classic Car Insurance
The Arch Barn
Pury Hill Farm
Towcester
Northamptonshire NN12 7TB
Tel 01327 810 607
Website www.hagertyinsurance.co.uk

HERO
Unit 13 Kenfig Industrial Estate
Margam
Port Talbot SA13 2PE
Tel 01656 740275
Website www.heroevents.eu

Historic Competition Services
Sint-Jansveld 5
2160 Wommelgem
Belgium
Tel +32 353 33 32
Website www.hcservices.be

Kingsbury Racing Shop Ltd
The Engine Test House
102 Bicester Heritage
Buckingham Road
Bicester
Oxfordshire OX26 5HA
Tel 07803 206536
Website www.kingsburyracing.com

NDR Limited
Mill House
119 Bushey Mill Lane
Watford WD24 7UR
Tel 01923 220370
Website www.ndr.ltd.uk

Rally Round
The Studio
Coachman's Lodge
Frensham Lane
Churt
Surrey GU10 2QQ
Tel 01252 794100
Website www.rallyround.co.uk

R.C. Moss Limited
Knotting Road
Melchbourne
Bedford MK44 1BQ
Tel 01234 709940
Website www.vintagebentleys.com

Stanley Mann Racing Team
The Fruit Farm
Common Lane
Radlett
Herts WD7 8PW
Tel 01923 852505
Website www.stanleymann.co.uk

Vintage Sports Car Club
The Old Post Office
13 West Street
Chipping Norton
Oxfordshire OX7 5EL
Tel 01908 644777
Website www.vscc.co.uk

Vintage Bentley Heritage
Hill Brow, Liss
West Sussex GU33 7NX
Tel 01730 895 511
Website www.vintagebentley.com

Appendix 5

Bibliography

Books

Automobile Racing, by Rodney Walkerley (Temple Press, 1962).

Bentley 4.5 Litre Supercharged, by Michael Hay (Haynes, 1990).

Bentley: A Racing History, by David Venables (Haynes, 2011).

The Bentleys at Le Mans, by J. Dudley Benjafield (MRP, 1948).

The Bentley Era, by Nicholas Foulkes (Quadrille, 2006).

Bentley Factory Cars, 1919-1931, by Michael Hay (Osprey, 1993).

Bentley Specials & Special Bentleys, by Ray Roberts (Haynes, 1990).

Bentley: The Vintage Years, by Clare Hay (Number One Press, 2015).

Blower Bentley, by Michael Hay (Number One Press, 2001).

The British at Le Mans, by Ian Wagstaff (MRP, 2006).

British Racing Green, by David Venables (Ian Allan, 2008).

Casino Royale, by Ian Fleming (Jonathan Cape, 1953).

Full Throttle, by Sir Henry Birkin (Foulis, 1934).

The History of Brooklands Motor Course, by William Boddy (Grenville, 1957).

Le Mans, by Anders Ditlev Clausager (Arthur Barker, 1982).

The Le Mans Story, by Georges Fraichard (Bodley Head, 1954).

Le Mans: The Bentley & Alfa Years 1923–1939, compiled by R.M. Clarke (Brooklands Books, 1998).

Le Mans 24 Hours, by Brian Laban (Virgin Books, 2001).

The Man who Supercharged Bond, by Paul Kenny (Haynes, 2010).

Montlhéry, by William Boddy (Veloce, 2006).

Moonraker, by Ian Fleming (Jonathan Cape, 1955).

Motor Racing, by Earl Howe and others (Seeley Service, 1947).

Motor Racing, by S.C.H. Davis (Iliffe, 1932).

Motor Racing and Record Breaking, by G.E.T. Eyston and Barré Lyndon (Batsford, 1935).

My Lifetime in Motorsport, by S C H Davis (Herridge & Sons, 2007)

The Other Bentley Boys, by Elizabeth Nagle (Harrap, 1964).

A Racing Driver's World, by Rudolf Caracciola (Farrar, Straus and Cudahy, 1961).

A Racing History of the Bentley (1921–31), by Darell Berthon (Bodley Head, 1956).

The Roaring Twenties, by Cyril Posthumus (Blandford, 1980).

The Sports Car, by John Stanford (Batsford, 1957).

Technical Facts of the Vintage Bentley (Bentley Drivers Club, 1955).

Tourist Trophy, by Richard Hough (Hutchinson, 1957).

Under My Bonnet, by G.R.N. Minchin (Foulis, 1950).

The Vintage Motor Car, by Cecil Clutton and John Stanford (Batsford, 1954).

Wheels Take Wings, by Michael Burn and A. Percy Bradley (Foulis, 1933).

W.O. Bentley – Engineer, by Donald Bastow (Foulis, 1978).

Magazines

The Autocar
Bentley Drivers Club Review
The Light Car
The Motor
Motor Sport

Index